Eirlys Thomas & L

SLOW WAL   THE
WALES COAST PATH

SLOW WALKING THE WALES COAST PATH

First Edition 2021

Text © Eirlys Thomas & Lucy O'Donnell 2021
Edit and layout: Shaun Russell

Jelly Bean Books
Mackintosh House, 136 Newport Road,
Cardiff, CF24 1DJ
www.candy-jar.co.uk

A catalogue record of this book is available
from the British Library.

ISBN: 978-1-913637-85-9

Printed and bound in the UK by
Severn, Bristol Road, Gloucester, GL2 5EU

INTRODUCTION

Deuparth gwaith yw ei ddechrau – Starting the work is two thirds of it.

We are walking in Wales in the winter. My cheeks are flaming red raw, tears are running down my face, and my nose is running. I can taste the salt on my chapped lips. We have walked into a storm.

I'm shouting, 'Why, Lucy? Why are we doing this?'

She can't hear; her body bent against the wind, hunkered down against the weather.

We are on the Wales Coast Path.

This eight hundred and seventy mile coastal walk is the longest of all of Wales's long-distance paths. A truly world-beating first for Wales. Wales is the first nation in the world to have a path following its entire coastline. The path was launched in 2012, the result of a formidable Welsh partnership of sixteen local authorities, the former Countryside Council for Wales, two National Parks, and the Welsh Government negotiating their way around the Welsh coast, joining up a myriad of existing routes and creating new where necessary. It is in its infancy and we are fledgling walkers.

From the age of five, I remember walking three miles between school and home every day. I figured over ten years I would have walked to the North Pole or even the Equator, but, if truth be told, I couldn't wait to get behind the wheel of a car. Lucy had on occasions flirted with ramblers, but had no huge commitment to the great outdoors. Nobody we knew would consider us 'walkers' by any stretch of the imagination.

City life was our comfort zone: theatre and cinema, concerts and exhibitions, wine bars and restaurants, with the familiar shout out at the end of the night 'taxi for Thomas' or 'cab for O'Donnell'.

Somewhere, deep in our subconscious, there was maybe a need to step off the social merry-go-round for a little while. So, with time on our hands and no commitments, we were ready for a new challenge...

It's difficult to pinpoint when we committed ourselves to walking the Wales Coast Path. It started as a chapter of incidences.

I was planning an adventure holiday in South America, and Lucy was planning a walk on the Camino de Santiago. Both of our fitness levels left a lot to be desired, so we decided to train for the up-and-coming trips.

Our training consisted of some short, local strolls along the coast. We discovered that walking the Heritage Coast in the Vale of Glamorgan and Bridgend was incredible. The tidal range is the second highest in the world after the Bay of Fundy in Canada, and this creates the most dramatic of seascapes.

On return, we both felt that the Wales coastline had as much, if not more, to offer than our overseas adventures.

We resumed our walks; short walks initially, but resolve stiffened, muscles strengthened, and despite blistering feet and the initial aches and pains, we found, to our surprise, that we were really enjoying ourselves; the pair of us looking forward with anticipation to planning and walking the next instalment.

In the words of John Cale, 'Time plays a role in almost every decision, and some decisions define your attitude to time.'

We had the time, and as far as attempting the longest path in Wales we thought, *Why not?*

From the early beginnings of our adventure, some things were set in stone. We wanted to experience Wales as we had never done before; enjoy ourselves, eat in local restaurants, see local sights and shop at every opportunity.

We set off to slow walk the Wales Coast Path.

We talked as we walked, sharing stories, learning more from the people we met and sought out. We learned about the landscape, the history and communities as we passed through.

Wales is a small country, but every mile has connections with people, towns and villages at the edge of Wales. The coast path inches around its *'ffin'* or boundary with the sea; in the walking the spirit of the place shines through, sometimes showing off a little, always a wonder, full of surprises and challenges. Our slow walk took a hundred days over eighteen months. We slow walked eight hundred and seventy miles from Chepstow to Chester and remain the best of friends.

We meandered a little 'off piste' when it suited us. We write to share the enthusiasm and inspiration that the Wales Coast Path gave us, in the hope that it will give heart and encouragement to any others who may dream of walking the length of the Wales Coast Path, or take the section from your own front door, taking in your local and most special part of the path.

We have become real ambassadors for the Wales Coast Path and share our tale with anyone who will listen about the natural gifts that we all have on our doorstep in Wales.

Eirlys and Lucy.

Chepstow Castle

South Wales – Chepstow to Swansea – 114.25 miles – 184km
Araf deg mae mynd ymhell – Go slowly, go far.

Chepstow to Newport Wetlands Centre

Chepstow is the starting point in South Wales for the eight hundred and seventy miles of the Wales Coast Path and, as two women reasonably new to walking as an outdoor pursuit, we face it head on!

We don't want to stride continuously along the path as if in a race, or to raise money, or in an effort to bag a long-distance path. We want to enjoy, get a little bit fitter and, who knows, lose a couple of pounds as we experience Wales as we have never done before.

The actual start or finish of the Wales Coast Path, depending on your direction of travel, is a little underwhelming: a small stone marker near the Old Wye Bridge in Chepstow. The same spot also marks the start or finish, again depending on your direction of travel, of the Offa's Dyke walk, a 177 mile walk from Chepstow to Prestatyn in North Wales – a story for another day. If you cross the Old Wye Bridge to the east, you are in England. Quite a thoroughfare!

Chepstow Castle is an essential diversion. The castle has over one thousand years of history and the oldest wooden doors in Europe. Its dramatic location, above the limestone cliffs of the river Wye, makes it a spectacular sight. The Wales Coast Path leads us through Chepstow's thirteenth century town wall, and takes in the Parish and Priory Church of St Mary, originally built alongside the castle in the eleventh century by William the Conqueror's Norman Lords.

Just before the 'old' Severn Bridge, which ironically passes over the river Wye, we use the tunnel under the M48 motorway. We are not overly impressed by the industrial site we take in along the way.

Onwards to Mathern Village, a conservation area, dominated by the lovely fifteenth century church dedicated to St Tewdrig, a medieval King of Gwent and Glywysing. St Tewdrig was injured fighting the Saxons and subsequently died, but he remains a hero in these parts.

We plough on through the marshes towards St Pierre, through very muddy fields and leg it when we see a large bull or bullock in the far corner. We discuss the benefits of wellington rubber boots or walking boots in this soggy terrain.

Walking around the corner of the St Pierre Golf Course, we chat to a group of young golfers also enjoying the winter sunshine. Newborn lambs in the field indicate that spring is on its way. The golfers are not aware that circuiting the golf course is part of the Wales Coast Path and a bit of banter follows. They're impressed with our ambition to walk eight hundred and seventy miles; we don't want to disillusion them by letting them know we'd only covered a few miles.

We take a breather in the village of Sudbrook. Built in the late nineteenth century for the workers on the Severn Railway tunnel, it is just over four miles long with two and a quarter miles running under the River Severn. The earth literally moves as the South Wales train powers through the tunnel on its way to London.

Today the Pumping House dominates the village, clearing over fifty million litres of water daily from the tunnel to prevent flooding and releasing it back into the Severn.

On this stretch we see two bridges in quick succession. The concrete feet of the now newly renamed Prince of Wales Bridge are as intimidating as they are awe inspiring. Brutal and overwhelming in size and scale, with constant traffic noise from the M4, the drivers are totally indifferent and ignorant of us cheery walkers far below.

We are impressed with the hardiness of the very few licensed fishermen who trudge out to cast their "Y" shaped lave nets on the River Severn to catch salmon. This is traditional fishing for hundreds, if not thousands of years. The current move to 'catch and release' might be the end of this way of life, with fishermen out in all weathers. It is the first, but not the last time we come across the conflicting needs of the Welsh environment and its people. Our early walks are day trips from home. Setting off early on winter mornings, we crunch through heavy frost and dull, cloudy weather. Trudging through muddy, cow pat lanes and sodden fields, sticking to our vow not to walk in wet weather, we are glued to the weather forecast. Yes indeed, we are fair weather walkers.

At the end of our walk, we summon a local taxi to take us back to the car. Trevor from Denzil Davies's taxi firm in Caldicot is a favourite. He keeps us entertained with local gossip all the way to our car parked in Redwick. He would have been happy to take us all the way to Cardiff, chuckling as he tells us that his wife would have to do the school run while he enjoys the high life of the big city. 'Probably get cold tongue for supper though,' says Trevor while he chortles infectiously. He is more enthusiastic about the possibility of a journey to Cardiff than Anna, our next taxi driver, who says that driving in Cardiff brings her out in a cold sweat, and on the outskirts of the city we can tell that is indeed true.

Trevor happily set us down in Redwick, not the least put out by the fact that we didn't want to go to the 'Big City'.

We are drawn to the Rose Inn. This local pub looks cosy and welcoming after a chilly morning's walk. We find a cat snoozing on a chair and a fire burning bright and warm. We order a comforting meal and I dash across the road to view St Thomas's Church. Some of the bells here date back to mid-fourteenth century. This is a quiet village and a good place to park up, even if you only want a short stroll.

The joy of walking in winter is that you can spot the birdlife quite easily. Great for the novice, as well as serious birdwatchers who turn out to be so friendly. We meet several twitchers, all packing serious cameras and binoculars. 'Morning, girls, nice day for a walk,' is the standard greeting. It is very cheering to be called girls as we walk, dishevelled and mud-splattered. We really embrace the experience and have our coffee break in a real bird hideout.

The Newport Wetlands National Nature reserve is a bird watchers' paradise. Our friendly twitchers give us a potted history. Apparently the wetlands were built on the ash covered industrial landscape of the old Uskmouth Power station. The intention was to provide a new habitat for birds displaced by the building of the Cardiff Bay barrage. We are reminded of the vulnerability of the landscape after spotting a plaque commemorating the twenty-two dead due to the Great Severn Flood of 1606/7.

The three lakes at the eastern end are the Goldcliff lagoons are Monk, Prior and Bec. Lucy is blown away as lagoons conjure up images of inlets in the South Pacific surrounded by coral reefs. She is surprised to come across them near Newport on reclaimed land, providing a variety of habitats, including wet grassland, hedgerows, scrub, reedbeds, water-filled ditches, reens, and the mud flats of the Severn Estuary. It is obvious from the enthusiasm of our new birding friends that this for them is a year-round attraction. In the spring the birds use the wet grassland to nest and rear their young, safe behind the lagoons. Several species of waders nest here, and we become familiar with a few of them as we make progress along the coast. Our favourite and instantly recognisable is the oystercatcher, with its distinctive red/orange bill and its pink/red legs.

During the autumn and winter months, the reserve is a vital pit-stop for migratory ducks and waders from Scandinavia and Europe, arriving in huge numbers. While the birds are quite happy to gorge on the creatures from the lagoon amidst the mud, sand and salt marsh, our feet are getting cold. It is time to move on.

(opposite) The start or finish marker for the Wales Coast Path with iconic 'dragon shell' logo.

Newport Wetlands Centre to Cardiff

We do not have high hopes for this next industrial section of the Wales Coast Path. Apocalyptic is probably a good description for some parts of the walk, but, surprisingly, this turns out to be one of the most remarkable days; the dark overcast weather adding drama.

We leave the River Severn and turn inland, walking along the banks of the river Usk, which flows down from the Black Mountains, through Newport town centre and into the Severn.

The first 'wow' of the walk is the Transporter Bridge. It is an industrial masterpiece, still in working order. It is only one of six bridges of its kind in operation in the world. Spanning the lower River Usk, it dates back to 1906. We don't cross the Transporter Bridge, although it is added to the list of things to do once we have completed the walk.

We head inland and cross the Wye on the outskirts of Newport using the City Bridge. At this point we call it a day.

Humming, *What a difference a day makes?* we are pleasantly surprised to find that yesterday's dismal weather has given way to bright sunshine. This totally changes our perspective of the industrial landscape. We are treated to a second look of the Transporter Bridge glistening in the sun.

The Waterloo Hotel lies in the shadow of the Transporter Bridge. It is an

original dockland pub and brothel. It has kept many of its original features and is decorated with many prints from yesteryear. We opted for a cuppa next door at Fanny's Café where you get a coffee; milky or not – none of your fancy lattes or cappuccinos. We like the lack of pretentiousness; breakfast looked good too!

The path leads us through the housing estate at Dyffryn, with some urban litter squalor adding a little grit to the day! Moscow is graffitied in huge letters on a neighbouring wall. Lucy wonders why someone has felt the need to make such a statement. Could we have entered a communist enclave? To her knowledge it was Maerdy in the Rhondda that had been called Little Moscow, the only town in Wales to have had a communist mayor.

Hats off to Newport Borough Council who have managed to link up the walking in their neck of the woods. Despite a bit of confusion, we appreciate the planning, and they have gone the extra mile, so to speak, to join up their pathways.

We are then treated to the glory of the coastal Gwent Levels: West Usk Lighthouse, the Rhumney Great Wharf, and Peterstone Gout. The latter having nothing to do with inflamed joints, apparently it is a flap which allows fresh water from the reens to flow out to sea.

The Rhumney Great Wharf is, for both of us, a mystery. What is the Rhumney Great Wharf?

We discover it is a high, wide grassy bank running along the edge of the coast between Newport and Cardiff. It looks like a raised path that could have simply been created for a stroll by the sea. The upper salt marsh is called the 'wharf' and the lower, towards the sea, is called the 'mudflats'. This can be viewed when the tide is out.

Excavations place the site as Roman. The discovery of ancient horse bones has leant some credibility to the suggestion that the Roman garrison at Caerleon might have grazed their horses here. As you walk along the sea defenses, looking inland at the low-lying fields, this landscape looks so vulnerable, while today's horses graze peacefully.

The Gwent Levels, which lie behind Rhumney Great Wharf, is entirely man made. The sea fortifications have been mightily enhanced over the ages. The Levels are criss-crossed by artificial drainage channels, known locally as 'reens'. It is a landscape more associated with the Netherlands than South Wales.

The salt marshes and levels are teeming with bird life. A Google search reveals regular updates from bird watchers, as we stand on an Atlantic migration route for all sorts of birdlife.

Anybody starting or finishing off at the car park by the Lighthouse Inn, next to a chalet park, should pop in and have a pint or a bite to eat. The staff and locals are as helpful as it gets, and the food is hearty and decent, and a major plus is the easy access to the shoreline and Wales Coast Path.

The mud flats and the jigsaw puzzle salt marshes complete the picture. Described as uninspiring by a few writers, we are, however, mesmerised by the landscape.

We are reminded of the fine balance between man's management of the landscape and cruel nature. The Bristol Channel flood of 1607 wiped out some three thousand people from Chepstow to Carmarthen. I guess we should ask, with global warming, rising tides and heavier rainfall, if it could happen again?

We follow the tidal basin of the Afon Rhymney and soon drop off the main road into the placid wilderness of Trederlech Park, with its fishing lake and bird watching opportunities.

We are dreading the stretch along Lamby Way as it approaches the largest refuse site in Cardiff. Thankfully, it is largely unobtrusive, apart from the sound of trucks churning away out of sight.

(opposite) Along the Gwent levels.

Cardiff to Llantwit Major

We skirt the Welsh capital city, Cardiff, during this walk. Much of it is along busy roads, even the guidebook tells you to 'grit your teeth' during the early stages.

Yet what glory comes into view. The Cardiff mudflats shine and shimmer in the sunshine as we are simultaneously over-shadowed by the industrial presence of Celsa Steelworks on the nearby East Moors Road. Our guidebook states that we will pass a small travellers' site. The signage is very haphazard and the mud beneath our feet sucks and slurps as we walk over ground, churned up with tyre tracks. We must look a sight from the road, as we bob up and down over and around the small hillocks. We stumble on the travellers' site; dogs are barking furiously as we hurry past!

Who knew Cardiff had a beach as well as a bay? Splott Beach or sometimes known locally as Brick beach. It gets this name from the demolition debris that has been scattered along the shore over the years.

We are almost immediately bowled over by a dog, quickly followed by the owner who says, 'So sorry, I've never seen anyone here before and I walk every day. I just let the dog run…' a beach made for one exclusive user!

We walk past a futuristic building, the Cardiff Energy Recovery Facility, which is the largest of its sort in Wales. Apparently, it converts 350,000 tons of non-recyclable waste into energy which can power up to 70,000 homes a year.

The low point of this walk is the depressing amount of litter in verges through Ocean Way and East Moors.

Cardiff Bay looks dazzling in the sun, reflecting off the copper tones of the Millennium Centre. We sit on the steps of the Senedd, the Welsh Government Assembly building to have our sandwiches, looking across at the red bricked Pierhead Building with its Baby Big Ben clock.

We walk over the Cardiff Bay barrage completed in 1999. During construction it was the most expensive engineering project in Europe. To Penarth Haven, passing through Penarth and its iconic Pier, easy to see why it was dubbed

'The Garden by the Sea' during the Victorian era.

Through Cosmeston to Lavernock, where we stop at the Captain's Wife pub for a shandy. Onwards to Sully Bay, Cadoxton and the route takes us towards Barry docks. The old dock's office is impressive. It is a 'calendar building'. It is called this because it has features which equate to the calendar, for instance: fifty-two marble fireplaces (weeks of the year) twelve porch panels (months of the year) and so on – you get my drift.

We must look very officious with our maps in see-through plastic polly pockets. One friendly local asks if we are marking out the route for the 10k race, and do we want money for charity; that is how friendly the locals are! We head towards Barry Island and have a coffee at Marco's café, particularly familiar to *Gavin and Stacey* fans. Walking around Barry Island, we love the bright-coloured beach huts, wide expanse of beach, and the fun fair. The vivid painted rides are silent and still in the winter sun.

On the headland we meet an old colleague. He takes one look at our polly pockets and comments wryly, 'That's a bit over the top'. It probably is for Barry Island. He tells us that he walked the Wales Coast Path in a matter of weeks, but this isn't the way we intend to go. Slow walking is our style, immersing ourselves in the detail.

We head towards the Cold Knap Point and reminisce about the outdoor lido, which is no more. It was said to have been the largest outdoor swimming pool in Wales. We moan about the price of progress, before getting nostalgic about Sunday school trips to Barry Island.

Porthkerry Park is a great stop, with its magnificent viaduct and very tasty bacon sandwiches at the café. We see a couple of planes coming into Cardiff airport, but they do not disturb our walking. There are two caravan parks on this stretch of coast, but neither do these add or detract from the walk.

We are slowly getting used to gritty, but really hate shitty. The narrow area skirting the Aberthaw Power station is splattered in dog poo, despite dog poo litter bins being provided by the local authority. It is an obstacle walk, and it is not nice! That said, the biodiversity site is pleasant, more bird life to enjoy, and the heritage coastline is always a delight.

To complete the walk, we leave one car in Porthkerry Park and drive the other car to the Llantwit Major.

CAUTION! If you are using two cars, do not leave the keys to one of the cars in the other one, as you will then either need to walk back to where you started or get a taxi! We opted for the taxi.

The last part of this section starts with a climb up the steps at Tresilian Bay, Llantwit. Silian was a Welsh Prince and Saint who reputedly held court in the third and fourth century. The walk is mainly over large fields passing the Seawatch Centre at Summer House Point, then winding down to Penry Bay, across Limpert Bay, both are pebbly and not easy to walk across.

(opposite) Penarth Pier.

Dunraven Castle and walled gardens.

Llantwit Major to Margam

The Wales Coast Path is seriously getting under our skin and we cannot wait to get on with the next section. My aversion to walking had been set to one side.

Llantwit Major is the site of early Christian settlement and we visit the eleventh century St Illtuds church, before starting the walk from Cwm Colhuw just outside the town. The Glamorgan Heritage Coast is a dramatic backdrop to this walk. Searching for Jurassic fossils on the beach has always entertained younger members of the family.

We come to a slipway where you catch glimpses of St Donat's Castle, now home to sixth form Atlantic College that houses students from all over the world. The newspaper tycoon, William Randolph Hearst, bought the house in 1925, and hosted amongst others Charlie Chaplin and a young John F Kennedy – such glamour in this little coastal enclave!

We visit the churchyard at St Donat's to check out some of Lucy's ancestors, before continuing our walk through some woodland, and then along the cliffs towards Nash Point Lighthouse, the last manned lighthouse in Wales. It was built in the nineteenth century and is currently grade 2 listed. There are some super self-catering cottages nearby. These would have been the lighthouse keepers' cottages.

We drop down steeply into the wooded area of Cwm Mawr and Cwm Bach, followed by a relatively easy cliff path to Whitmore Stairs, an impressive seventy metre cliff with a large rock outcrop beneath. The path goes close to the cliff edge at Cwm Nash. Burial remains from the fourteenth and sixteenth century have been discovered here. It is possible that it was a graveyard for drowned sailors or for those who could not afford a plot in the churchyard. More remains were found in 2014, when storm damage uncovered further body parts!

Our next stop is Dunraven Castle with its walled garden and we are glad to see the toilets. The castle has origins in the Iron Age. Caractacus or Caradog had a home here when he fought off the Romans. Then came the Saxons, the Normans, the Welsh Princes and Owain Glyndŵr, before becoming a hospital for the Red Cross during the First World War. The original garden was built in the sixteenth century, but later altered. It is a very peaceful spot for a picnic.

The following day we leave the Pelican in her Piety pub and head down river, taking a sideways glance at the Norman remains of Ogmore Castle. We reach Ogmore Beach and stop for a coffee at Coffi Pig, a converted horse box selling decent coffee.

We don't remember much after this. It is all a bit hazy. As we chat, we forget to read the signs and, all of a sudden we are straddling an unfenced cliff. We can't look down. It looks too dangerous. Scrambling up the slope on hands and knees seems the safer option. We right ourselves at the Barn at West Farm and continue in a more orderly fashion, before once more reaching the charming Dunraven Bay, again stopping for a respite. The two of us sniff the air like Springer spaniels. It is said that a woman haunts the garden, and if you get a whiff of her perfume, then disaster is bound to follow. We've had our disaster for the day, so are glad when we don't detect anything.

This is a lesson learned. Be aware of your surroundings, don't hurry along the path, stop and enjoy the view. Also, pay attention to signposting, and where these are minimal, resort to a guide book or the Wales Coast Path App (if you have signal).

A week later, we are back in Ogmore-by-Sea, fully recovered from our experience. This time we linger at Ogmore Castle. Dating from the twelfth century, it sits above the River Ewenny.

Not particularly familiar with tide tables, we are reminded that, in future, we should check before fording estuaries on our walks. More by luck than judgement, our timing is perfect. Riders from the nearby trekking centre are making their way down river.

We go across at the stepping-stones, gingerly making our way so as not to get our feet wet at the start of the day. We head through the village of Merthyr Mawr, with its beautiful thatched cottages, before reaching Merthyr Mawr sand dunes and the nature reserve. The dunes are among the tallest in Europe, at around two hundred feet, and are surprisingly difficult to walk up, stretching the calf muscles as you do so.

The scene changes as we reach Porthcawl, passing through the huge static

caravan park, Trecco Bay. Some say it is the largest in the UK. The owners of the caravans take obvious pride in the ornamental decorations in their small gardens. We suspect local rivalry as each one is more flamboyant than the last. We are particularly taken with the tortoise display.

Gill, who joins us for this part of the journey, hilariously recounts her misspent youth at Coney Beach funfair with Lucy.

Soon we cross Sandy Bay and reach the harbour at Porthcawl. We head to the Pier Hotel for coffee and tea cake. There is an easy walkway alongside the prestigious Royal Porthcawl Golf Club, founded in 1891 by a bunch of Cardiff businessmen. As well as the golfers, a small group of surfers are out to sea on Rest Bay, a hardy lot. The yellow washed Sker House can be seen from the path. There has been a house on this site for nine hundred years. R D Blackmore in 1872 wrote the novel *The Maid of Sker.* He eventually went on to write Lorna Doone. Sadly, there was a real maid of Sker House, a young lass called Elizabeth Williams. She was forced into a loveless marriage by her father Isaac Williams, while she was madly in love with a harp playing carpenter.

Sker Point was the tragic scene of the disaster which struck the US built Samtampa, a 7,200 tonne steamship. It got caught in a gale on the 23 April 1947. Eight lifeboat men from the Mumbles and the thirty-nine sailors from the Samtampa were killed.

Sker beach is unofficially a naturist beach, but is usually deserted apart from a few horse riders, and a single dog walker... all clothed.

The beach runs alongside the Burrows, from Porthcawl to Port Talbot. It glistens in the bleak winter sun as the sky darkens, and we race to complete the walk before it rains.

(above) Looking back at Aberavon Sands and Port Talbot.
(opposite, bottom) Tennant Canal.

Margam to Swansea

The walk from Margam has the constant, dominating backdrop of Tata Steel works. Even walking through Kenfig Burrows alongside the nature reserve (a site of special scientific interest) you still glimpse the works in the distance.

On the day we walk this stretch, the workers from Port Talbot steel works are voting on an offer made by owners Tata to accept a reduced pension scheme in return for keeping the steel works. They accept the offer.

We share memories of Port Talbot. The times when I used to return from working in London and the steel works were lit up with the furnaces belching smoke and fire. I feel as if I am almost home, although it will be hours before we reach Fishguard Station.

Lucy has other fond memories of her days at St Joseph's comprehensive. Secret afternoons off school on the beach before the end of term, trying all sorts of experiments to get an early summer tan. Parties overspilling on to the beach as day turns to night.

Then, by chance, our taxi driver mentions that he was at the same school as Lucy and knows some of the same people. Many stories are shared on the way back to our car. We learn to love these random encounters and conversations. Earlier that day we chat to a lady walking her corgis. She knows a mutual friend. In the world it is thought that there are six degrees of separation. In Wales I reckon it comes down to about two degrees.

The sun shines as we walk along Aberavon Beach, a magnificent three mile stretch of sand, a playground of many a Sunday school trip. The beach looks manicured, with people dressed up, promenading and chatting together, as they enjoy the sea front.

Leaving Aberavon beach we head over Baglan Burrows, a mix of salt marsh and brackish marsh, reed beds, and shrublands. The dunes are gouged with tyre marks from illegal motorbike riders. I can't understand the attraction, and it must play merry hell with the plant and wildlife.

We go past the power station and pipeline, and soon see Brunel Tower, named after the designer of Briton Ferry docks, Sir Mark Brunel. There is not much left to signify how busy this dockland was in the nineteenth century.

After some banter with three middle-aged cyclists we cross the Briton Ferry bridge. Lucy recounts the time when her dad had a car accident on the bridge, and her mother only found out about it when she saw the car on the news. You can only imagine the consternation in the O'Donnell household.

Before we head under the M4, we sneak a look over the edge of the Briton Ferry bridge to have a good look at what exactly sits in that little triangle between the M4 and A4, some moored boats, a couple of houses, and a fire station.

We marvel at the pillars shoring up the M4, wondering how much concrete has gone into the foundations. You don't fully appreciate the engineering that goes into our roads until you walk over and under them!

Following the A483 for a while, we are glad to turn off this busy road towards Jersey Marine and eventually the quieter stretch of the Tennant Canal, previously known as the Glan y Wern, which was used to transport coal.

(above) Approaching Swansea Marina.
(below) Ashlands woods.

We skirt around the Park and Ride car park, before ending up in the SA1 area of Swansea. The change in the area is remarkable. It's been ages since either of us were last here. The once derelict docks have been transformed into an open modern marina and bayside area.

Crossing the Trafalgar Bridge, both of us feel pleased at having completed the South Wales section of the Wales Coast Path.

Lucy stubs out her cigarette as we finish this first stage of our journey. I have lost count of the number of times Lucy has given up smoking over the years. The methods she has used and the expense of it all. This time though the stubbing out was final, painless and free.

Brimming with success, we fully deserve lunch at the Grape and Olive, appreciating the views out to sea from the high-rise location, while raising a glass to our accomplishments to date and the next instalment.

Three Cliffs Bay.

Carmarthen Bay and Gower 124.25 Miles – 200 km
Ychydig yn aml a wna lawer – A little often will do much.

Swansea to Rhossili

Watery sunshine greets us in Swansea and we set a fast pace along Swansea Bay, joined by our friend Enikö and dozens of walkers, joggers and cyclists. Apart from interacting with our birding friends, we have, to a large extent, enjoyed the South Wales path in glorious isolation. We aren't used to dodging the health fanatics making the most of the fitness trail to the Mumbles. It seems as if the whole student population of Swansea is waking up to spring. It is good head-clearing weather, and the daffodils, snowdrops and crocuses on either side of the trail are a reminder that winter is on the wane.

The Mumbles is an iconic stretch of Welsh coast, with the late nineteenth century pier and the gentle curve around the headland to Gower. Generations of students and locals will have hazy memories of the Mumbles mile. At its peak there were twenty-six pubs, and the rite of passage would be to drink at least half a pint in each pub.

The seasons might be changing but we are not happy to see the storm clouds gathering as we reach Gower. Bad weather has been predicted but not until nightfall. Our pace quickens, but the storm hits hard and fast as we reach Langland. We struggled onward to Pennard Cliffs. It takes an age with high winds, rain, hail and mud.

My cheeks are flaming red raw. Tears are running down my face. My nose is running. I can taste the salt on my chapped lips. We have walked into a storm. I am shouting, 'Why, Lucy? Why are we doing this?'

She can't hear; her body bent against the wind, hunkered down against the weather. We are on the Wales Coast Path and we haven't seen the last of the winter!

Bruising hail stones hit us hard in the face. Turning a corner, the wind catches my jacket and, for a horrifying moment, I think I am going to go flying over the edge of the cliff.

The Gower Peninsula was the first Area of Outstanding Beauty in Britain, designated in 1956. It is renowned for its glorious scenery. Heads bent against the wind and wet, we certainly are not experiencing Gower at its best.

We can see the all-weather surfers are still out to play, testing the waves in the sea below. While walking in such inclement weather has been quite exhilarating, we unanimously decide to call it a day.

Approaching Southgate, Lucy spots the Dandelion café. It is about to close, but happy to accommodate latecomers. Lucy immediately orders a large glass of red wine. We gently steam in the corner, and with wet weather gear drying off nicely, the café owners kindly stay open until our taxi arrives, giving me plenty of time to enjoy my hot chocolate with a tot of brandy.

This is the day that Lucy finds out that her walking gear cannot withstand a Welsh deluge. 'Wet to the bone,' she says. It is also the day that our vow only to walk in fine weather is turned on its head.

Bracing ourselves against the wind and rain.

Next day, dried out and keen, we find Gower shrouded in sea fog. We are doomed yet again not to see the outstanding views. The distant vistas are soon forgotten in the sheer enjoyment of early spring, May blossom in full glory, a yellow blanket of primrose in the woods, and a carpet of bluebells, already in early bloom.

By the time we reach Three Cliffs Bay, the mist has disappeared and we head for Pennard Castle. Legend has it that this twelfth century castle was engulfed in sand because the owner at the time refused to let the fairy folk dance at his wedding.

To add to the spookiness, the castle is also home to *Gwrach y Rhibyn*, the witch of the mist... She wasn't out to catch us today as we are now 'walking on sunshine' – which led us nicely into a song.

At low tide, we shadow the stream at Pennard Pill and cross over the stepping stones. Wales Coast Path takes you through Oxwich Burrows, the beach sadly is out of sight most of the time.

The more challenging part of the walk comes after we pass St Illtyd's Church, just outside Oxwich. I find old churches fascinating; here in the corner of the graveyard there is a dried up well. The story has it that a white horse, *ceffyl dwr*, a water horse has been seen disappearing into the well. More ghostly Gower tales!

Heading into the woods there are steps, up and down they go, a total of four hundred and forty. We are glad to have rounded Oxwich Point and we are on the home run to Horton, only to be confronted by a diversion. It isn't a long detour, but it is the last thing you want to see near the end of a hike.

The next leg of the walk is from the National Trust car park at Rhossili and back to Horton. We head down towards Worm's Head. It is high tide and it cannot be reached. It takes its name from the Nordic 'Wurm' meaning dragon.

We aren't able to get down to Paviland cave either, due to the tide. Paviland is where the skeleton known as the Red Lady of Paviland was discovered in 1823. The so-called red lady has subsequently been identified as a man. The skeleton has been dated to be 29,000 years old. After today's walk, we feel as old as the skeleton, as there are many ascents and descents on this leg of the Wales Coast Path.

The sun burns through and we regularly stop to take in the landscape. There is a heady, pungent smell of the yellow gorse in the air worthy of a Jo Malone candle.

The sea crashes on the rocks. There is a haunting sound of the bell on a lone life buoy way out to sea, the sun sparkles on the ocean. A fishing boat comes into view, a bumblebee hums as it dives into the gorse flowers. This leads us into another chorus of '*Walking on Sunshine*, oh, oh'.

All is well with the world as we reach Horton and complete the South Gower section of the path.

Whitford Point Lighthouse.

Rhossili and Penclawdd via Llanmadoc

An early start in bright sunshine, we walk towards Rhossili Bay along the north coast of Gower, approaching Rhossili from the west. We believe that this will give us the best vantage point for the beach and Worm's Head.

Our tactics to get the most out of the day is to use two cars. We are becoming well versed in selecting our start and finish points. For instance, today we start off by driving two cars to Rhossili, (end point of the walk), parking one car in the National Trust car park, then driving to our setting off point – Whitford Beach Car Park at Llanmadoc. At the end of the day, we pick up one car and drive to the other. Sounds complicated, but it is not. In the more remote areas, where public transport is at a premium, it works for us.

Membership of the National Trust comes in very handy. There are several National Trust car parks in Wales, particularly around the coast, which are free to members.

We stop for coffee at the Cwm Ivy café, before heading off in the direction of Rhossili. The friendly owner of the Cwm Ivy café opens early for us, and we have time to browse in the shop for locally crafted items, but we are diverted by the smell of freshly baked scones: delicious!

We walk around Whitford Burrows, through the dunes, to reach

Whitford Point. This walk takes in Whitford Point lighthouse, with a walk along the beach, and then a climb up Hill Tor, rather than taking the alternative shortcut avoiding the Whitford Point all together.

Two people walking rarely share the same emotional response to a place – but we do here – it is enchanting.

The scenery is bewitching: the blend of colours, the light and shade through the trees, coupled with the aroma from the rich mix of marsh, dunes and beach and pine. Alongside this is a clear view of the bright, blue sea across to Whitford Point lighthouse and the only cast iron water lighthouse left in Britain. It was incredibly special.

It is difficult to put into words, but the Wales Coast Path becomes a personality from this point on. Most people would say we are being fanciful. The path has already been cruel and kind to us. This is the moment we become totally captivated by our experience, the path's ability to engender such a primitive joyous response is quite overwhelming, unexpected, and rare in today's frenetic world.

Rhossili Bay does not disappoint. We are happy with our decision to approach the beach from a westerly direction, with the tantalising Worm's Head as an end goal. It has been a constant landmark, a distant dragon emerging from the water, and we now have the 'Wurm' in sight.

We experience the exquisite pleasure of taking off our boots and walking bare foot in the sand on Rhossili beach, followed by the pain of squeezing them back on for the final mile to St Mary's Church in Rhossili. Then staggering into the Worm's Head pub for refreshments and being delighted by the Dylan Thomas quotes over the bar.

Another day and a false start. We leave Llanmadoc and head towards Penclawdd. When we get to the Groose – a dyke traversing the marsh – there are diversion notices. The sea wall collapsed in 2014, and a decision by partnership bodies regarding the best solution to the problem has yet to be taken.

Inspecting the damage, it is indeed wiser to retrace our steps and change our route. Unfortunately, the tide hasn't quite reached its lowest ebb, enabling us to cross the marshes. We take the red route, the indicator for the alternative route when the tide is high.

Muddy underfoot, with pleasant blue sky and some cloud, we make our way across the Landimore salt marsh, skirting Weobley Castle, a fourteenth century fortified Manor House.

We meet five ladies from London, checking their Land Ranger maps, and give them the benefit of our recent experience and diversions. We are beginning to sound as if we know what we are talking about.

Squelching our way along, past curious sheep and horses to Llanrhidian marshes, the landscape seems primeval. We elaborate our storytelling with fantastic tales about creatures from the deep rising from the marsh.

Reaching a dung heap covered in toad stools triggers off a distant

(above) Horses near the Llanrhidian marshes.
(opposite) Through the pines by Whitford Point.

memory of the '*Tylwyth Teg*', the fairy folk who roam these parts. Turning a corner, we half expect to see a group of pixies in red and green dancing a jig, but as dusk approaches our fanciful tales fade away and they don't seem quite so funny anymore, telling ourselves we aren't superstitious, while casting surreptitious glances over our shoulders.

Our walk through to the village of Crofty is uneventful. Passing the processing plant for Penclawdd Cockles, before reaching the car. Penclawdd is the centre of the cockle picking area – an old photograph shows a woman and her donkey on the sands in Penclawdd. The women have now been replaced by men on tractors licensed to pick!

We are delighted to see them as a starter on the menu (cockles that is, not men) at the Railway Inn, Penclawdd that evening. My main course is Burry Port Mussels. Simple local food, cooked well, what more could you want after a long walk.

(above) Fair night in Burry Port.
(opposite, bottom) Signposting the Amelia Earhart flight.

Carmarthen Bay to Penclawdd to Burry Port

Carmarthen Bay is not an area we know as well as the path already travelled. The transformation of this area from its industrial past is a revelation.

Much of the walk is along the Millennium Coastal Path. It replaced the huge power station and heavy industry that dominated this area, and is now a playground for walkers, cyclists and golfers – a mostly flat, traffic-free route covering approximately thirteen miles of leisure walkways, cycle trails, several nature reserves, and a Nicklaus designed golf course at Machynys.

We don't pause too long at Loughor Castle, even though it does date back to the twelfth century, but detour to the Wetfowl and Wildlife centre. Someone has recommended that we should pop in and see the little egret (which is protected there). We learn that the centre houses some sixty thousand birds.

The old Stradey Park rugby ground has given way to a housing complex, while the goalposts are topped with the traditional 'sospan fach', as a nod to the tinplate industry in Llanelli.

The walk is helped along by brilliant sunshine, sparkling seas, blue skies and the very friendly locals.

Our days out are becoming too long to travel from home, complete a day's walk and then drive back. We start experimenting with short breaks. We explore travel options, but as we frequently set off in different directions at the end of our walks, it is best to travel in separate cars. This leaves us with a certain amount of guilt during the whole adventure. We still want to do the best we can for the environment!

We stay in a very 'tidy' apartment by the harbour in Burry Port, booked through AirBnB, a booking service we use regularly while walking the coast of Wales. Our 'home away from home' overlooks the beach with stunning views of the Worm's Head and Gower in the distance. It is also within a stone's throw of the Parson Pickles factory, housed in an old tinplate building. We wonder if they have a factory shop.

In Burry Port, references to Amelia Earhart regularly appear around the town. She flew with two companions from Trepassy in Newfoundland in June 1928 and landed in Burry Port, taking just over twenty-one hours. She only had fifty gallons of fuel left when she landed. Subsequently, in 1932 she became the first woman to fly across the Atlantic, before disappearing without a trace on a flight in 1937.

Staying in Burry Port, our imagination is fired by the tales of *Gwyr y Bwelli Bach*, men of the small hatchets. These men were a tight knit band of local families who looted the cargo of the many shipwrecks along this coast. Survivors of the wrecks must have been horrified, having survived the cruel seas, to then be confronted by this determined bunch of reprobates.

Changing out of our walking gear, we wander into Burry Port and look for the travelling fair we spotted earlier. These fairs have always been a big attraction in Welsh village life. Twice a year they arrived in our local villages much to our excitement. As teenagers we had dire warnings from our mothers to stay away from the fair boys, they were thought to 'play fast and loose' with the local lasses.

It is only 7pm and the fair is shut for the day. The last ride was at 6pm on a Saturday night! The parents of teenagers in Burry Port can sleep comfortably in their beds. No 'playing fast and loose' here. The fairground lads are litter picking around the site. We tut tut and mutter 'it wouldn't have happened in our day'. Who knows, it may be a change for the better.

Our alternative is to engage in a mini pub crawl, where we are entertained by locals singing bawdy rugby songs, ending the evening with a meal at Whitfords, a restaurant recommended by our singing friends.

(above) Shipwreck at Cefn Sidan sands.
(opposite, bottom) Kidwelly Castle.

Burry Port to Carmarthen

Nothing stirs in the early morning as we leave the quiet, coastal town of Burry Port. It is hard to believe that coal, copper, silver and lead used to be shipped from what is now a pretty marina.

In contrast, Pembrey Country Park is bustling with dog walkers and cyclists. This is a great space for outdoor enthusiasts; it even has a ski slope. Hidden away are the remnants of one of the largest armament factories in Britain operated during World Wars I & II. The workers became known as the 'Canaries' as some of them turned yellow from handling the munitions.

The seven miles of Cefn Sidan (Silky Back) sands makes this an easy stretch to walk. We find a map listing the shipwrecks along this shore I give up counting after seventy wrecks. Some can still be seen along the shore. Josephine's (wife of Napoleon) niece is at rest in the local church after the sinking of La Jeune Emma. These are the kind of random facts we glean along the way.

We are slightly confused as we leap into summertime; the clocks have changed, but we are still out on the path at 7am! A footpath closed sign at the start of the walk soon clears any cobwebs.

A word of advice, if you prefer walking up steps then cover this section from the Kidwelly end, and if you prefer going down steps then approach the walk from Ferryside – it may be easier on your knees.

We know Kidwelly Castle well. It is featured in the opening scenes of the film *Monty Python and the Holy Grail*. It is a Norman castle and sits watchfully above the estuary of the Gwendraeth Fach. St Mary's parish church is also impressive and is open to visitors. There is a nursery rhyme called *Hen Fenyw Fach Cidweli* referring to an old lady from Kidwelly selling black sweets or liquorice. It is my turn to burst into song.

There are not many stop-off points, but there is a pub in Llansaint. This little village was built back in the fifth/sixth century around a cemetery. There are over three hundred place names in Wales prefixed Llan, and usually followed by a named saint, but Llansaint translates as Church of the Saints.

With a fresh breeze and early morning sunshine, even the farms we walk past are quiet. Dozy sheep stare at us with a startled expression. The countryside appears still, but as we watch hares race across the fields. A heavy overlay of dew covers the ground, and blackbirds sing out as we walk. We resolve to set out earlier in future to capture the dawn chorus.

Passing several farms, there is one steep sixty step drop, a pleasant but not spectacular walk. The main drawback is a chunk of road walking. This is rather hard on tired feet and is away from the coast.

From Ferryside, mentioned by Gerald of Wales in 1188 as the ferry crossing to Llansteffan, we walk northwards to Carmarthen. Where is the ferryman when you need him?

Today we had opted for a taxi at the end of our walk. We have found taxi drivers a font of local knowledge, gossip and quite economical so far. Eddie, our friendly taxi driver was very obliging, but a whacking £35 fare had us rethinking our travel arrangements for the next day.

(above) Llansteffan Castle.
(opposite, bottom) Lucy's muddy boots.

Carmarthen to St Clears

The day starts at the large fish sculptures on the outskirts of Carmarthen. We previously walked up the Tywi estuary to Carmarthen, we are now heading down the river Tywi towards Llansteffan. I find estuary walking exasperating as it is only a short distance across the estuary from Ferryside to Llansteffan.

Today is the day that all our walking 'tools' give up on us. The app, map, the guidebooks and the path signs don't quite match up. We also have four human opinions, having been joined by our friends Enikö and Kim. A chat with a friendly local Welsh speaking farming family soon puts us right. They couldn't be more helpful when they learn of our adventures and dilemma. A bit of a wobble, but we are soon back on track.

Kim and Enikö pick fresh wild garlic for our evening salad, as we wonder why more people don't forage for free food. They make sure that they pick far away from the path, so that the young leaves are not contaminated by dog fouling.

The section between Carmarthen and Llanstephan is a lot of road walking, not our favourite surface. Views of the coast could only be seen at the end of the walk.

Llansteffan beach is pretty as a picture. There are lots of young families on the beach, enjoying the brisk, if bleak weather.

A detour up to the castle is a bit of a challenge at the end of a day's walking. Llansteffan Castle ages from the twelfth century. It flick-flacked between the Welsh and the Normans, both vying to take control of this strategically placed fortification over the centuries. It is good to know that today it is back in local ownership.

Much of the walk up to St Clears is very mucky and once again the Wales Coast Path takes us away from the coast for the most part. The ground is sodden, our boots sinking into mud, and brown splatters all over our wet weather trousers. It was so mucky that Lucy's new boots were well christened and, at one stage, a boot is sucked off her foot, and a walking pole gets stuck.

The image of Lucy trying to rescue stick and boots with her perfectly manicured pink nails will stay with us for a long time. We share a giggle as she hobbles out of the mud, with a very muddy foot, and boot and sock in one hand.

As we walk around a busy roundabout, we hear a car toot its horn repeatedly. Looking round we see friendly Eddie, our taxi driver from Saturday with a cheerful, 'Still walking, ladies?' He disappears down the road.

More mud follows, and we gratefully stagger into the Santa Clara pub in St Clears, where the local builders, enjoying a swift pint, have a great laugh at our expense.

Laugharne is our home for the weekend. We are incredibly happy to shed our boots, but unable to resist a walk around Laugharne to find the moon is full and there is a light mist over the town – very Dylanesque!

In the evening we dine at Arthur's, a very friendly eatery in Laugharne, while the salad prepared by Kim and Enikö from the wild garlic is kept for another night.

Laugharne Castle – Castell Talacharn.

St Clears, Pendine and Amroth

I wake early. As I load my boots into the car, I see a notice pinned to the window.

DO NOT PARK HERE.

I double check the street signage, no laws broken. Before I drive off an irate woman comes out and berates me for parking in HER space. I thought it best to be very apologetic!

Other Laugharne residents have been very friendly and helpful, so I wasn't about to condemn the whole village on the basis of one confrontation. Besides, I love Laugharne, with all its Dylan Thomas connections.

We are tracking back to St Clears in the car. It is the first day for us to wear t-shirts; signs of warmer weather ahead...

Leaving the A4066, we enjoy the peace and quiet along the river Tâf. On reaching Laugharne, we follow the Dylan Thomas's Birthday Walk leading down into the charming township.

We stop to chat with a lady walking her dog. It turns out she is Sonja Brown, the well-known Laugharne Castle custodian who knew Ms O'Donnell from her time working in Cadw. There is a lengthy catch-up before we set off again.

Staying in Laugharne, we have plenty of time to meander to the Dylan Thomas Boat House and Shed, and St Michael's Churchyard to visit the poet's grave.

From Laugharne to Pendine is not that spectacular, peppered as it is with an indifferent walk alongside the A4066. It is time to share memories:

Lucy in her younger days wanted to show off her new jeep to her parents. There followed a trip to Pendine Beach. If it was good enough for a land speed record, then it was good enough for a test run. Mum and Dad O'Donnell were in the back seats. Driving down the beach they wondered why they were being chased by a jeep full of soldiers. They were pulled up and escorted back to a sign which read: MINISTRY OF DEFENCE. DO NOT ENTER: LIVE FIRING. Lucy and parents lived to tell the tale.

The world land speed record was broken here five times. The rivalry between Sir Malcolm Campbell and J G Parry-Thomas is the stuff of legends. J G Parry-Thomas died here in 1927 when he crashed trying to beat Sir Malcolm's record. The car he was driving called Babs would rust away under the sand until 1969, when it was recovered and restored. It is now in the Pendine Museum of Speed.

The Amroth to Pendine section of the walk had been completed earlier in the year while we were both holidaying in Pembrokeshire with our respective families. It was quite an experience as the walk coincides with Storm Doris.

We gave up on the first attempt, but the next day as Doris still simmered, we set again. By the time we arrive at Gilman Point we have experienced four seasons in one day.

Marros sand is a lengthy stretch of beach, where the wreck of Rover can be seen. The schooner was beached in a force eleven gale back in 1886.

Further along the headland is Morfa Bychan, bought by the National Trust to avoid any other developments along this stretch of coast. It was here, a large deployment of troops, rehearsed the 1944 D day landings.

At Gilman Point, there is a vicious wind blowing. The path zigzags uphill tempering the steep incline, but at three hundred and ninety-five feet we are rewarded with a view across the Carmarthen coastline. Before we start the descent, we look back over our shoulders towards Tenby and Caldy island, and ahead in the distance the Gower comes into view. Below is the golden stretch of Pendine Beach, home to numerous land speed records.

Our walk ends with an all-day breakfast in the Point café, the only place open in Pendine. The entertaining and chatty owner has relocated from Merthyr. The toilet facilities are restricted because the water is 'off'. We could use them on a promise of only 'number 1s and no toilet paper'. We just love the Valleys' way.

The tide recedes but leaves behind,
bright sea shells on the sand.
The sun goes down, but gentle
warmth still lingers on the land.
The music stops, and yet it echoes
on in sweet refrains....
For every joy that passes,
Something beautiful remains.

(above) Lucy spots a naturist.
(opposite) The words ring true for the Wales Coast Path.

Pembrokeshire Coast Path 174.50miles - 280.50km
Dôd yn ôl i fy nghoed – Coming back by trees or finding your life balance.

Amroth to Stackpole Quay

By now, we have covered the South Wales, Gower, and the Carmarthenshire sections of the Wales Coast Path. We start on the so called 'Mother of all Paths', the Pembrokeshire Coast Path.

Opened in 1970, this path is well established and expertly managed. Overall, it is what it says it is, a path that hugs the coast.

Our base for this adventure is the ideally placed East Trewent Farm in Freshwater East. In extremely comfortable surroundings, we thank our pleasant hosts for the full Welsh breakfast, and set off on our journey.

We had completed the walk from Saundersfoot to Amroth at the tail end of Storm Doris and we're now heading towards Tenby along the beach at Saundersfoot as the tide is out. The path heads up steeply from the sands, continuing to rise and fall for much of the walk. We meet a couple of walkers, who warn us of the climb ahead. They say, 'Very glad we are walking in this direction'. What do they know? I ask, 'Have you walked from Chepstow?'

But it seems they did know and the ascent from Waterwynch goes on forever.

We eventually catch tantalising glimpses of Tenby, with its pretty harbour and views out towards Caldy Island. We stop for a particularly good coffee in Café Vista, and enjoy the scenery, while we chat to a couple who were both on their third marriages! If at first, you don't succeed...

The Wales Coast Path signs are not very visible about the town, but our guidebook sets out a clear route to South Beach. The red flags are flying at the Penally range: FIRING IN PROGRESS. We find that the MOD presence is at odds with the beauty of the place.

We detour into Penally as directed by the signs. The signs give clear instruction on how to proceed and one sentry clears our way up the outer boundary of the range. We are met at the top by a truly angry sentry who proceeds to tear a strip off us. Confusion reigns, but luckily for us no bullet wounds!

We catch up with some walkers who spend a week every year walking the Wales Coast Path. We figure we would be well into our dotage if we only walked one week of the year. Our conversation is interrupted by a group of young cadet soldiers carrying full packs, racing along the path. We admire their strength and stamina.

We follow the limestone cliffs, up and down, until we reach Lydstep Beach and head gratefully through the caravan park and up the hill to the car park at the end of our trek. It has all gone very well, and our thoughts turn to a pub meal, and the inviting beds at our B & B.

At Lydstep point early the next morning, a couple of lads are messing around on the high vertical limestone cliffs with a sheer drop. For one moment we think they will fall over the top and shout a warning, but our voices are carried away in the breeze. They do realise their stupidity and stop shoving each other. Pembrokeshire, a whole different experience.

To Skrinkle Haven and onwards towards Presipe Bay, stopping only to take in the views and chat to a sweet family who had been recommended this beach as one favoured by the locals. Good on them we say, for avoiding the popular crowded beaches, which are easily accessed by car.

Descending to Manorbier Beach, we pass the King's Quoit, an ancient 'cromlech' burial chamber.

Several volunteers are working together to keep our coast clear of rubbish. We have repeatedly seen the mounds of rubbish that beach cleaning volunteers have collected for a council pick-up, much of it brought in by the tides, but also left by uncaring visitors. A note from a volunteer replying to a letter of thanks has been left on a bench. Unsung heroes –

many thanks. Hats off to Keep Wales Tidy and people who care about our environment.

Manorbier Castle, a Norman-style Manor House overlooks the beach. Gerald Cambrensis (or Gerald of Wales) was born here in 1146. Gerald travelled Wales and the continent in the twelfth century and wrote in detail about the experience. His writings are some of the earliest to describe Welsh life. Famously he wrote, 'If the Welsh would be inseparable, they would be insuperable' meaning that the Welsh, unlike the English, fight for their country not money, but they have a habit of fighting too much amongst themselves. We debate whether the quote is relevant today as we walk along.

Crossing the stepping-stones, we curve around East Moors Cliff to Swanlake Bay. It is not an official nudist beach, but we do cross paths with a chap wearing only a beige sweater. It is a difficult moment. On a cold day it must be a nudist dilemma, to go topless or bottomless!

Arriving late afternoon at the Longhouse, Freshwater East, we are delighted that Sunday lunch is still being served and we tuck in with gusto, before setting off, chanting the nursery rhyme *The Grand Old Duke of York* as we once again march up a hill to Greenala Point, and then downwards towards Stackpole Quay.

Tenby with its colourful houses.

The Green Bridge of Wales before a massive chunk fell into the sea.

West Angle Bay to Stackpole Quay

We are by now well-versed in what we call the 'top and tail' walks. These are relatively short walks taken on the days we travel to and from a destination. Basically we plan our walks to allow for a short stretch on the first and last day of our stay. In keeping with our philosophy of 'slow walking', our enjoyment isn't impaired by rushing to our walking destination, or being too tired to drive home. It is also helped when sections of the path are too lengthy to complete on a single day – usually we 'tail' the walk off on a subsequent visit.

At West Angle Bay, we are pleased to have free parking, and find a café called the Wave Crest, where we enjoy locally caught crab.

Out to sea, Thorn Island, with its coastal artillery fort is intriguing. It was built as part of the nineteenth century defence against invasion, due to the proximity of the Pembroke Naval Yard and Milford Haven.

This coast seems to have been heavily defended. Out on the headland are the remains of the small East Blockhouse Fort built in the sixteenth century, while Rat Island and Sheep Island are mere rocky outcrops.

Shipwrecks abound on this coast. In 1878 the Loch Shiel went down with a cargo of whisky, gun powder and beer. This was spirited away by the locals. It could be said to be the Whisky Galore of South Pembrokeshire.

As we get closer to Freshwater West there are several steep ascents and descents, with some sixty-five steps to climb near Black cave.

Freshwater West is noted for sunsets and film sets. *Harry Potter and the Deathly Hallows* and Russell Crowe's *Robin Hood* were both filmed here. It is a glorious stretch of beach.

We complete our top and tail walk here. In the morning we parked a car in the shelter of the Burrows, knowing that we could enjoy the sunset at the end of the day.

It is Easter, and in Freshwater West we trip over a memorial service commemorating the tragic loss of lives from WWII. On Easter Sunday, 26th April 1943, two landing crafts were making their way from Belfast to Falmouth. A vicious storm resulted in seventy-two Royal Marines drowning off the coast. A further six men died from the Royal Navy volunteers of HMS Rosemary. They were trying to set out a line to save the shipwrecked men.

We pause to join in the ceremony and talk to several of the ex-servicemen present.

We then check out the Pembrokeshire Beach Food Co., selling delicious freshly-cooked local seafood and seaweed snacks from their wee café. We stop to look at the seaweed drying hut, before moving on towards Castle Martin, a Ministry of Defence firing range. Live gunnery exercises take place here, and we are careful to check out the shooting times before going ahead with our walk.

We follow our guidebook instructions. For some reason the signage is confusing. Despite being aware that there was no shooting planned, we still find it quite unnerving. It is such a pity that a large section of the peninsula is inaccessible due to military manoeuvres – and the constant warning signs are also a bit of a downer.

We eventually find the sign for the Green Bridge of Wales and Elegug (guillemot) stacks. On our way we chat to Edward Dunn, a landscape artist from Llanglydwen, who has escaped from the stiff breeze on the headland into more sheltered ground.

We detour to see Flimston chapel, set in the middle of the firing range. We were unaware at the time, but you can get a key from the guardhouse to access the building.

From the Green Bridge of Wales through to St Govan's Head, the scenery is achingly beautiful, and well worth the discomfort of the firing range. Young rock climbers are taking advantage of the sheer drops, but most surprising is a young man on a mobility vehicle precariously parked on the edge of a cliff. Lucy thinks it is joyous seeing him at one with nature. I am concerned that he is on his own and may be in some difficulty. We join him for a chat. It turns out he is waiting for a friend who is investigating the Devil's Cauldron, a collapsed cave.

We still have enough energy to walk down to St Govan's Chapel, named after a sixth century Irish saint, although some say that Govan is a derivation of Gawain, one of the mythical knights of Round Table fame. There may have been a hermitage here in the sixth century, but this chapel dates mainly from thirteenth century.

At this stage I decide to take off my boots as they are new and beginning to pinch. It isn't a good idea as gorse bushes flank the way.

Beyond Broad Haven it is a huge relief to reach Barafundle Bay, frequently featured in best beach awards for the UK and worldwide. The steps up from Barafundle Beach are punishing, particularly if you are only wearing socks.

We were intending to detour from Broad Haven to Bosherston Lilly Pools, but with the shadows lengthening we push on to Stackpole Quay, once used to bring coal in and send limestone out by sea. Our day ends at the National Trust tea rooms and car park.

St Govan's Chapel.

A welcome seat for weary walkers.

West Angle Bay, Pembroke and Milford Haven

Following a three week break, we are back on the path. We decide to walk this stretch in two sections, both leaving from Pembroke town. The first leg from Pembroke to West Angle Bay and the second leg from Pembroke to Milford Haven.

Starting at Pembroke Castle, birthplace of Henry Tudor, Henry VII, we immediately pause for coffee and retail therapy at the Cornstore. We shelter until the rain stops before we embark on the fifteen mile walk from Pembroke town to Angle. To date this is the longest distance we have walked in a single day.

We head towards Monkton, where a woman is berating her little boy in no uncertain terms. The little boy will be awfully familiar with four letter vocabulary long before he is of school age!

We rest at Pwllcrochan, a very tranquil setting. The church here dates from 1342 and it is locked. We stroll through the churchyard and down to a reed bed in the hope of spying some otters. Even though we wait patiently, they are not going to favour us with their presence.

The day's walk is overshadowed by the refinery and jetty as we head full tilt to Popton Point.

We have a drink at The Old Point House in Angle, but as dinner is not being served until much later, we hurry to West Angle as the daylight is fading, and we are yet to find our cottage for the weekend.

While tackling the stretch from Pembroke Town to Milford Haven, the day starts badly. We miss the coast path signs coming out of Pembroke town. Retracing our steps, we head back to Food at Williams on Pembroke's main street for some decent coffee. Lucy regales me with her experience of visiting Pembroke Castle and the vivid description by the guide of Oliver Cromwell's siege of Pembroke Castle in 1648. The woman must have been a great guide as the memory has stayed with Lucy for a long time.

My momentary annoyance at missing the signs passes and we resume our walk in good spirits.

We headed into Pembroke Dock, passing an old disused fort, and shuttered shop fronts making the town look run down – such a shame considering its proud past. The wall sculptures provide a great insight into the rich history of the port as we descend to the Martello Tower on the Quay. The Irish Ferry between Pembroke Dock and Ireland is in port as we walk onwards across the very windy tollgate bridge, looking down on the Aberdaugleddau estuary.

Pausing to check our bearings, we are accosted by an Australian walker. She is very insistent that she knows the way. We follow but let her stride ahead because we aren't totally convinced. After a few hundred yards with our Australian friend out of sight, we retrace our footsteps and are soon on the right track to Neyland.

Our feet are beginning to ache from all the road walking. We pause to take our shoes off, with Brunel's statue looking stonily on.

The village of Llanstadwell is a pleasant distraction with its pretty church and roadside flower displays. Beyond this point is a plethora of high metal fences, bleak and forbidding. We walk under the massive wind turbines. The noise they make is reminiscent of the opening scene of Apocalypse Now. Thwack, thwack, thwack as they spin in the wind sounding like Huey helicopters.

We walk over high metal bridges, the LPG pipelines and onwards through farm fields to the edge of the river, over the Black bridge, keeping a wary eye open for the traffic here. Beyond Pill to the Rath and downhill on Hamilton Terrace.

We pass the Lord Nelson Hotel named after the Admiral himself, who had made a speech there in 1802. Our conversation centres not on Nelson but Emma Hamilton, wife of the local landowner Sir William Hamilton, who had a longstanding affair with Admiral Nelson. Such scandal.

At the end of this lengthy walk, our feet are smarting. Even with new boots, it is worth checking the insoles. After hundreds of miles walking they are threadbare and our feet suffer.

(opposite) Pembroke Castle.

Pembrokeshire's stunning coastline.

Milford Haven, Dale and St Martin's Haven

This stretch is covered by three walks from Milford Haven to Sandy Haven, Dale to Sandy Haven and St Martin's Haven to Dale. The weather is changeable. Rain, sun, rain. We have to adapt our plans. We decide on a short walk from the more sheltered Milford Haven to Sandy Haven joined by our friend Gill. The grass is high, wet and needs cutting back, and my skin is smarting from some stinging nettles. We walk beneath the gas pipeline leading to the refinery and, before we know it, we are approaching Sandy Haven. An early finish! Soon we are having a nice lunch at The Bar in Milford Haven Marina.

The sea is sparkling in the morning sunlight as we head out of the small village of Dale towards Musselwick, over the steppingstones. This is perfect timing as the tide is far out.

We go up a path and through woods to Monk Haven, with its high castellated walls. The name suggests an ancient monastic settlement, but the high walls are far more recent, a boundary to the nearby estate.

Waiting for Lucy and Enikö (a new friend for a new day) to catch up, I get talking to a local bird watcher who insists on walking with me a little way to point out the nesting peregrine falcons. He leaps up on a hedge and pulls me up after him. He then complains that I am too short, whereupon I fall backwards into a gorse bush.

He then gives up on me.

We do keep meeting people who are passionate about their interests all along our journey.

Despite my prickly bottom, I get to see the circling falcon, if not the nest!

Arriving at Sandy Haven beach, the tide has turned. We had been so aware of the earlier tide at Musselwick, but had dawdled for far too long to cross over to Sandy Haven. We can no longer ford the gap and have no alternative but to tear our eyes away from the nearby shore, and head inland for a four mile walk to Herbrandston.

We take a quick stop in the pub, and with some friendly guidance from a local, we eventually get to Sandy Haven.

Metatarsals mangled from road walking, we are grateful for a vicious June storm that comes in overnight putting paid to our plans for the next day.

When the wind drops the next day, it is beautifully clear, but the rains are coming in at 2pm, necessitating an earlier check out from the cottage, cars to pack up and a need to get to our starting point sooner rather than later.

St Martin's Haven is the place where the boats depart for Skomer in the summer. Skokholm Island is a hazy speck in the ocean, some two and half miles from shore. Both are bird and wildlife havens. Skomer Island, closer to the shore, is home to half the world's population of Manx shearwaters. It is the Atlantic Puffins who arrive on Skomer Island around April that are the real draw. They are the photographers' dream bird!

We quickly reach the very stunning Marloes Sands and the tidal island of Gateholm. The headland is very noticeably featured in the film *Snow White and the Huntsman*. A computer-generated castle was added to the island in post-production.

Passing an old airfield, we drop down the valley into Westdale Bay.

We reach St Anne's Head and lighthouse, only to find the access gate to the path blocked by a cow rubbing her nether regions against the gate. There is no moving her, despite trying all my Pembrokeshire bred knowledge of 'cowersion' tactics. The other frisky cows in the field are attracted by the noise and make their way to the gate. We have no option but to circumnavigate the field until we find another entrance!

The next point of interest is Mill Bay, where in 1485 Henry Tudor landed with his French allies and set forth to do battle at Bosworth Field, defeating Richard III and taking the throne of England.

Onwards to the West Blockhouse, a garrison built in 1857 for thirty-four men and one officer, now owned by the Landmark Trust, it provides extremely comfortable holiday accommodation.

Beyond Warwick point, with its huge navigation pillar, we get to Dale Point, reaching the road and eventually down through the woods to Dale village, passing a sculpture workshop on the way.

Then it rained!

St Brides Castle.

St Martin's Haven to Nolton Haven

This walk exceeded all expectations. It offers some easy walking mainly along clifftops – around twelve miles in total. After parking at St Martin's Haven, we head up the coast passing Musselwick Sands towards Nab's Head. The path was overgrown around East Hook, with some nettles – a prickly start.

The headlands stretch out endlessly before us, blue on green on blue. Sky, land, sea.

Tower Point provides a distinctive landmark. It is a large sandstone stack and, as we continue on, we catch glimpses of St Brides Castle, built in 1833 by William Charles Phillips, and added to by the sixth Baron Kensington in the early twentieth century.

St Brides Castle became a sanatorium called Kensington Hospital, and I remember visiting when my mother became an inpatient for some nine months. The place smelt of disinfectant and old-fashioned Mansion polish, the kind you were able to buy in a tin. The windows and doors were always open, while the place still retained some of the grandeur of the fine country house built for Lord and Lady Kensington. When my mother was allowed to sit outside, I loved the formal gardens with the vivid rhododendrons in May.

It was a confusing time for a teenager. I remember my father, who was very much the head of the family, was like a lost soul. I was about to sit my exams, having been offered a place at nursing college. My sister was getting married and I vividly remember visiting my mother in our wedding finery. I was in a sulk as nobody had told me my bra strap was showing when we had our official photographs taken. I did feel quite the princess though; walking up the polished staircase to see my fragile mother, who was delighted but quickly worn out by our visit. We were all adrift, my mother who was always in the background had a far bigger influence than she would have ever imagined. In her absence I turned from a shy child into a wilful teenager, who simultaneously had far too much freedom and responsibility. Thankfully, my mother came home. This episode made me realise I was not cut out for the nursing profession.

Subdued, after trading emotional family memories, I take one last look at St Brides Castle, today transformed into luxury apartments, before reaching St Brides a tranquil sheltered haven. Nearby is St Briget's church named after Bigid of St Kildare who travelled to Wales with St David in the sixth century.

At Mill Haven we encounter the grass cutters. The path will be cleared for future walkers. Enticing us on are the views of Broad Haven beach in the distance, before the scenery changes quite radically as we move onto Burrough Head, entering a cool woodland, providing welcome relief from the heat.

Lucy and I talk about the Pembrokeshire murders. In the late 1980s a middle-aged couple from Oxford had been brutally shot on the path. The killer wasn't caught until 2011. We can't quite get our head around a killing in such a peaceful spot.

Lost in conversation, we are startled by a loud 'BOO' from a man who had previously walked by and is now sitting on a bench. It scares us witless; we scream and then we all laugh, but we move on very quickly!

A young man and his father hasten by to catch the walkers' bus. They are late. 'No chance,' we mutter.

We try our best to fit in our walks with the local shuttle buses, but don't have much success. We talk to walkers who have used the Puffin and Strumble Shuttle and Poppit Rocket and loved them. We wander down into Little Haven and walk across the beach to Broad Haven, where we stop for a snack and cooling drink. Walking out of Broad Haven we remark on the Sphinx-like rock known locally as Shag Rock.

It takes us no time to find the dramatic rock formations called Settling Nose and Haroldston Chins. We are both impressed with the accessibility track leading from the roadside parking to the viewpoint at the Chins. It is certainly a wonderful place to provide access, as the views are insurmountable.

As we passed the Druidston Hotel, Lucy recounts something that happened there previously. She remembers wandering back to her eco hut after dinner. She was shaken by the sound of deep breathing. Without a

(above) Haroldston Chins.
(below) Horse and bike, really?

torch she raced along the cliff edge to the hut, only to find cows grazing peacefully there in the morning. We laugh about this all our way down the track, until we see the roof of the 'Teletubby House' or Malator, the earth house designed by Future Systems.

Looking across at sandy Druidston Haven, there is quite a lot of soil erosion. A bit scary; it is a reminder of the power of the sea and weather.

Eventually we descend into Nolton Haven, passing the church and into the free car park with toilets. It's amazing how important WC stops can be during and following a long walk.

After a day's walk, we welcome the crisp bed linen and the fluffy white towels at the Old Cross Hotel, St Davids. The steak and a nice bottle of Malbec at dinner caps the day off nicely. It makes a very pleasant change from self-catering, comfortable and convenient as that might be.

Solva.

Nolton Haven to Solva

Early morning, before breakfast, I walk down the steps towards Glyn Rhosyn and St Davids Cathedral. Mist hangs over the valley. As school children we learned that three pilgrimages to St Davids used to equal one to Rome and that the bones of St Davids are held here in a casket. St Davids itself is little bigger than a village but because of the cathedral it is designated a city. The smallest city in Britain no less.

I race back to the hotel for a hearty breakfast with Lucy, before making our way to Nolton Haven.

This turns out to be a relatively easy walk – just under eleven miles. Mainly over clifftops but with some steep steps. We still hate steps. Lucy hates going down and I loathe going up, give us a natural incline or decline any day!

In hindsight, if this is the first walk you complete on the Pembrokeshire Coast, or the Wales Coast Path, it probably wouldn't be considered 'easy'. It is all relative, by now we have walked a couple of hundred miles and we are considerably fitter than our first short encounters with the path. I would suggest it is best to read your guidebooks and maps carefully to judge the terrain. Then make your own judgment on whether the walk is easy or tough.

We set off, but quickly return to the car as the heavy mist has turned into a drizzle. Nolton Haven is a bit of a scrappy shingle beach and even the surfers don't look happy with the weather.

It is too early for the Mariner's pub, so we sit in the car gazing gloomily out to sea. The first break in the mizzle and we are up the incline and on the headland. It is breezy!

Our first surprise is evidence of coal mining. Something you wouldn't associate with the modern day Pembrokeshire coast. Trefrane Colliery was opened in the 1850s and records show that in 1896 it employed thirty-six miners and eight surface workers. Reimagining life below ground for a miner is bad enough, but in a seam that leads out to sea – unbearable.

Further into the walk, we reach the two mile stretch across Newgale Beach. The tide is out, and we make our way down to the sands, an easier and more satisfying way than along the busy road.

It does mean a scramble at the end, up the large pebble wall, deposited by the great storm of 1859. This forms a natural barrier between the beach and the roadway. We head to the Duke of Edinburgh for a swift drink, non-alcoholic and, more importantly, a toilet-stop.

We stroll up the hill out of Newgale. There are quite a few steps on the next stretch to Cwmbach, but easy walking to Porthmynawyd. I have never been to this beach before, but I do vaguely recall it being mentioned in *The Guardian* as one of Wales' top ten secret beaches.

It nestles into Dinas Fach, one of two headlands. We quickly reach Dinas Fawr (d*inas* – city, f*ach* – small and f*awr* – big).

We come to a pretty valley named after Elvis, the Irish Saint who baptised St David, not as in Presley.

More steps at the Gribbin before eventually passing the limekilns, dating from late eighteenth to early nineteenth century, into the pretty harbour of Lower Solva, straight into the Harbour pub for a swift pint of lime and soda!

If you like your pint after a long walk, there are at least three pubs within a hundred yards!

Trefane Colliery.

Early morning detour to St Davids Cathedral.

Whitesands to Solva

Rising gradually from Whitesands, passing the lifeguard station, beyond a couple of houses and we are out on the clifftops to Porthselau. Our goal, thirteen miles on a sunny day. Well signposted, without great inclines and declines and unsurpassed scenery every step of the way.

The sheer rocks beyond Point St John are impressive. With Ramsey island nature reserve in the distance, we make good time to St Justinian lifeboat station. There has been a lifeboat station there since 1839. And the old one sits alongside the new station. It is also the embarkation point for trips to, from and around Ramsey.

We slow our pace. This is too beautiful a day and too glorious a setting to hurry. We reach the most westerly point in Wales out on the remote Treginnis Peninsula.

From Pen Dal-aderyn, looking down on Ramsey Sound, we head towards Porth Lysgi, named after an Irish saint who landed there, before reaching the tiny harbour of Porth Clais – a drop off point for pilgrims and saints travelling from far and wide to visit the very holy St Davids.

We don't meet a saint, but instead Lucy's neighbour, Neil. Such a small world!

The harbour is surrounded by limekilns. Lime has been used on soil in these parts since the 1600s, but the kilns came later. Limestone imports were burnt with culm to create a powder for farmers to improve the land. This was mixed with sand to make mortar for buildings. Farmhouses in the area and beyond were also whitewashed with lime.

On the other side of the harbour we climb steadily, then across St Non's Bay with its crumbling cliffs. We detour off the coast path to take in the six hundred-year-old St Non's chapel and St Non's well. Non was the mother of St David, Wales' patron saint.

Rounding the corner at Pen y Cyfrwy we walk towards Caerfai Bay, with its gentle curve, clean sands and caves to explore!

The path is easy to follow. We particularly like that on the Pembrokeshire Coast there are small white plaques with the grid reference and names of each bay clearly marked. It makes it so much easier to pinpoint our location on a map, should we need rescuing!

Caerfai gives way to Carn Bwdi Bay, leading to an easy walk at Morfa Common, dropping down to a bit of a stream below Nine Wells.

The remains of three Greek boats wrecked in 1981 can still be seen at Loch Warren.

You can see Upper Solva a long time before you reach the corner and turn down towards Lower Solva. It is a bit of a hash of a route down a sunken path to the harbour, hard to believe that in the eighteenth and nineteenth century this was one of the busiest ports on this coast.

David Gray lived in the village from the age of eight, and we won't mention the large stinky fish washed ashore!

(below) St Justinian.
(opposite) St Non.

(above) Melin Trefin.
(opposite, bottom) Porthgain.

Abercastle to Whitesands

There is only limited parking at the small jetty in Abercastle, with an honesty box located just before we access the path. We make a swift detour to Carreg Samson, a five thousand-year-old Neolithic Dolmen, it is only a quarter of a mile away from the path, and the diversion does not use up much energy.

At Trefin we see the remains of a corn mill, putting me in mind of a favourite Welsh poem by Crwys:

(Nid yw'r Felin heno'n malu Yn Nhrefin yn min y mor).
The mill is not grinding tonight in Trefin at the edge of the sea.

The poem talks about the death of the miller and eventual dereliction of the mill. Lucy is learning Welsh, and the poem provides a good illustration of how the Welsh language can mutate.

We cross a small footbridge passing the old mill at Aber Draw. The water – the power source – forcefully spills down the slope to the sea. We go up a tarmac path and road, then through a gate, all clearly signposted. The path goes very close to the cliff edge at times.

We reach a white beacon, before descending into Porthgain.

Porthgain is a small harbour, once used to ship slate quarried in both Porthgain and Abereiddy. The slate gave way to the brick industry. It is now a protected area, with small art galleries, the Shed fish restaurant, and the Sloop pub, where we stop for a drink.

We triple our water intake on this walk. It is so hot! We still end up with sausage fingers and toes! Plenty of water is needed. Particularly when the chances to fill up water bottles are few and far between. It is pretty remote once you are past Abeireiddy.

Steep steps take you out of Porthgain.

Lucy earwigs on a group of four hovering at the top of the steps. They are animatedly discussing the future of the prime minister of the time – Theresa May! For the duration of our Wales Coast Path experience the conversations around us, on the path in pubs and restaurants, are dominated by Brexit and Donald Trump. In my lifetime I have never heard so many political discussions. Everybody has a view and much of it is polarised in one direction or another.

We pass above Traeth Llyfn and swiftly onto The Blue Lagoon, where the Red Bull diving championship are being held, before reaching the beach at Abereiddy.

This coast is busy with people coasteering, canoeing, diving; young and old walkers, fathers carrying toddlers on their backs, all making the most of this wonderful natural landscape.

The path dips at Porth y Rhaw. We then steadfastly go up and across Penberry Hill. Steep and rocky in parts, we shoo grazing horses away, so we can make our way through a gap between rocks. Heading towards St David's Head, the moorland opens out ahead. It is rough ground here; the heather is just about coming through, turning it into a purple haze.

Once past Penllechwen headland, the path is less prominent. We pick one of the several routes across the common. If in doubt stick to the right! At one stage we opt for the middle and work our way back to the path as we come down into the sandy, sheltered beach at Porthmelgan.

Thankfully, a broad and very visible path leads us down to Whitesands Bay.

Strumble Head to Abercastle

On the Pencaer Peninsula, Strumble Head in spring is divine. The headland is jam-packed with birdlife. From, not knowing our goose from our gander, we are still on a 'birding' learning curve, but are pleased we can identify a few. I think this is the most attractive scenery so far. The spring flowers are nature's multi-coloured carpet, the iconic lighthouse and the interlinking bridge makes it picture perfect.

Today we walk from Stumble Head to Abercastle.

We stock up with enough food and drink for the day. This stretch is quite remote. It takes you over several rocky outcrops, with an uphill climb to Pwll Deri, where there is a remote clifftop youth hostel.

The joy of these North Pembrokeshire walks is that there are great views inland as well as the coast.

We come out onto the roadway and walk past the memorial stone to Dewi Emrys, a Welsh poet whose most famous poem was entitled Pwll Deri, written in North Pembrokeshire dialect.

'A thina'r meddilie sy'n dwad ichi, Pan fo'ch chi'n ishte uwchben Pwllderi.'
'And these are the thoughts that will come to you when you sit and look at Pwll Deri.'

At Pwllcrochan, we run into a jolly group of walkers, led by Mr Peter Broomfield. They hail from Scotland. We talk about our adventures on the path and compare the merits of walking in winter and spring. Mr. Broomfield suggests that Welsh sheep poo is much smellier than Scottish sheep sh*t. His argument is that this is because there are more sheep in Wales on lusher pastures than in Scotland, therefore the poo is smellier. We are not going to do a smell test, even though there are enough samples to choose from on the ground. His friends tell us to be sure to mention him by name in our writings.

We decide that, on the whole, walkers are genuinely nice people.

We head towards the twin beaches of Aberbach and Abermawr, both beaches are backed by pebbles. Looking at the beach in Abermawr, I can't help thinking that Brunel was a bit off the mark in thinking he could turn this area into a port, but who am I to judge this magnificent engineer. The first thing you notice as you descend onto Aberbach is the vivid green marsh leading onto the pebbles.

Between here and Pwllstrodur the sea is strewn with little rocky inlets. It is an easy walk alongside the man-made stone wall, nicknamed 'the Great Wall of China'.

Eventually we reach Abercastell, a small working fishing village, with a tiny jetty and limited parking, but no shops or café, so we drive to nearby Melin Tregwynt for some food and drink, and some shopping. We end up buying a ridiculous amount of presents for the family.

It is worth noting that the local Strumble shuttle bus stops in Abercastle and Melin Tregwynt.

DEWI EMRYS
1879 – 1952

"A THINAR MEDDILIE SYN DWAD ICHI
PAN FOCH CHIN ISHTE UWCHBEN PWLLDERI"

(above) Jellyfish floating on the sea.
(opposite) Dewi Emrys memorial at Pwll Deri .

Strumble Head to Goodwick

It is a delight to return to Strumble Head for our walk northwards towards Goodwick.

At Porthsychan, Lucy thinks she has spotted a seal. I am short-sighted and am convinced it is a buoy, but a few minutes later we hear a plaintive call and way below us we get a clear sighting.

We also spot several jellyfish, looking like an alien species in the clear blue waters.

A little cottage appears on the headland at Penrhyn.

A memorial stone commemorating the last invasion of Britain is seen near Carregwastad. An elderly American, Colonel Tate landed in 1797 led the invasion of one thousand two hundred French men. They were thwarted by local women dressed as soldiers.

The Last Invasion Tapestry can be seen in Fishguard recounting the story. Jemima Nicholas is the local heroine of the invasion, rounding up twelve soldiers single handedly and locking them up in the church. We make a note to check out The Royal Oak pub on the roundabout in Fishguard, as this is the unlikely place where the peace treaty with France was thrashed out.

We walk through Harbour Village. I stop to talk to an elderly gentleman surrounded by wee dogs. He offers us a drink, but we move onto the final descent into Goodwick, treating ourselves to a delicious Sunday lunch at the Rose and Crown.

(above) Lower Town Fishguard.
(opposite, bottom) Cwm yr Eglwys.

Parrog, Newport to Goodwick

The Pembrokeshire Coast Path opened in 1970 and has been well trodden ever since. The good weather in late spring means we have experienced some wonderful walks. Fortune favours the brave!

From the Parrog beach near Newport to Cwm yr Eglwys is perfect, with pungent smelling blue- bells, gorse and a bright blue sea. The Parrog literally means a flat base for unloading boats.

Cwm yr Eglwys is an attractive hamlet on the sea front. The West Wall of the twelfth century St Brynach church is still standing after being abandoned following the Great Storm of 1859. We make time to sit and enjoy the tranquil setting. The first snack break of the day.

You can take a shortcut here to Pwllgwaelod. The Wales Coast Path, however, goes around Dinas Head, and so do we. Slightly more challenging but not difficult.

At Pwllgwaelod, we stop at the Old Sailor pub for liquid refreshments. I still regard North Pembrokeshire as home, even though I haven't lived there for decades. It is a Welsh thing! Happy memories as a teenager of drinking in the pub after a game of tennis in nearby Dinas Cross or sunbathing on Newport beach, then walking to Pwllgwaelod for a BBQ. Happy days.

The Old Sailor dates to 1593. The walls would have witnessed some smugglers in their time. In the 1980s, the locals became curious about a bunch of strangers flashing their cash and paying for drinks out of bags full of money. There had been tales of some strange movements in Slipping Bay near Moylegrove. The local curiosity and gossip led the police to investigate and to the arrest of a large global network of drug smugglers. Operation Seal Bay still gets talked about in pubs.

The Wales Coast Path leads you up an incline in front of the pub and from here to the Old Fort in Fishguard. The Old Fort was built around 1751 and from here canon fire was released against the French during the 1797 invasion forcing them to seek a landing further west.

Lower Town Fishguard looks pretty in the afternoon sun. *Under Milk Wood* featuring Richard Burton and Elizabeth Taylor was filmed here. *Moby Dick* was also filmed in these parts. My sister had an evening job at the cinema in Fishguard and often talked about how Hollywood took over the town. A touch of glamour in the far west of Wales.

The hill leading down from the Old Fort is steep as is the incline to Fishguard town, and we gratefully turn off accessing Marine Walk from Bank Terrace leading to a pleasant stroll into Goodwick.

Parrog, Newport to St Dogmaels

A leisurely stroll from St Dogmaels to Poppit, followed by some thirteen miles of the most challenging stretch of the Pembrokeshire Coast Path. This stage is variously called strenuous, gruelling, exhausting. It is all of these.

I remember the day that my pre-teen nephew and I set off from Newport to complete this walk without enough water, no food, no sun cream and wearing shorts and trainers. Thinking it would be a doddle. It took hours and the child's mother was ready to send out a search party, we had taken such a long time.

There is little scope to leave the path on this section apart from walking inland from Ceibwr Bay to Moylegrove. This stretch cast a huge shadow over my head since the start of our adventure. I convinced myself that I would fail on this section.

My starting point was to make sure this time we were well stocked with supplies.

We leave Poppit Sands and climb past the Youth Hostel, looking over our shoulders we can clearly see Cardigan Island, and the whole of Cardigan Bay.

We pass a farmhouse near Allt y Coed campsite and go through the farmyard. As we do so, we chat to a farmer bottle feeding some lambs. He jokingly says that we might want to wipe our feet on the way out of the yard. It is a bit mucky.

We climb around Cemaes Head and then after that we are up and down, first Pen yr Afr, then further climbing up to Pwllygranant. We take time out to sit on a bench overlooking Ceibwr Bay, knowing there is worse to come. Goods used to be ferried ashore here in days gone by. These days it is a place to try out a bit of sea canoeing and seal watching.

The scenery is simply spectacular, words can't do it justice, and neither can any photographs truly represent the beauty of the walk.

Pwll y Wrach (or the Witches Cauldron) is an interesting feature – a collapsed cave. It is one steep climb after another, followed by descents, then up and down again. Horses graze to the very edge of the cliffs, worryingly at times looking as if they are suspended in mid-air. It is, of course, an optical illusion; the animals are sure-footed and used to their coastal feeding ground.

A clear view of the main Newport Beach takes us by surprise. It looks wonderfully near, but we are not there yet. There is a difficult rocky descent, followed by more steps and stiles before reaching the car park and toilets. The path continues across the golf course, passing a limekiln until we reach the road. We cross over the bridge and follow a sign that takes us to the Parrog.

We are grateful to be picked up after the walk by my big brother and family.

In Scotland they bag a Munro, we have been bagging coast paths in Wales. Today we conquered the enthralling, rugged, captivating Pembrokeshire Coast Path, all one hundred and eighty-six miles from Amroth to St Dogmaels.

Hurrah, we head for home feeling very satisfied.

Snowdonia and Ceredigion Coast 137.50 miles – 221.28 kms
Bob un cam, cer ymlaen – every step moves you forward.

St Dogmaels to Mwnt

Completing the Pembrokeshire Coast Path is a biggie. We are not defeated by the 'Mother of all paths'. We are glad that we've built up our fitness level on the less challenging South Wales section, before reaching the west coast.

Our journey takes us north, but in our usual pragmatic fashion, we head south from Mwnt. In the evening we stay with Will and Eileen, my brother and sister-in-law at Eglwyswrw (frequently pronounced by English friends as Eggs of Sorrow), located a few miles south of St Dogmaels.

Mwnt is a favourite spot for dolphin spotting and sunsets. The tiny whitewashed Church of the Holy Cross dates from the fourteenth century. It nestles below Foel y Mwnt. This peaceful setting is at odds with the bloodshed of 1155 when the Flemish tried to invade. Sul Coch y Mwnt – Mwnt's Bloody Sunday is commemorated in the month of January.

Lucy's friend, Louise Williams, based her *Bake-Off* design on this little church and when it collapsed on the show it was her turn to leave the kitchen.

Disaster…

We both totally admire anybody who would go on a televised cookery programme.

Baking is not one of our skills.

The beach at Mwnt is sheltered on all sides, with a National Trust car park and toilets – two big pluses for walkers.

One thing we miss on this stretch is the grid references on the signposting. This is so obvious on the Pembrokeshire coast. The Ceredigion path logo dominates with few Wales Coast Path signs.

The path veers inland through a field and then down through Ferwig towards Gwbert with views across to Poppit Sands. Following the track alongside the main road, we soon reach a turn-off. This takes us through fields teasing us with views down onto the river Teifi.

Crossing a road to some fields takes us further away from the river. We follow the signs until we pass a sewage works, and eventually we drop down into Cardigan.

I buy a painting from a lady in the Guildhall. This was the first civic building in Britain to be built in the Gothic style, very daring in its day. The artist tells us she lives on the coast path near Llangranog. We jokingly say we will pop in for a cuppa later in the week. Leaving the painting to be collected we walk through the main street.

Reaching the newly renovated walls of the twelfth century Cardigan castle overlooks the Teifi River. We leisurely view the manor house and have coffee at the 1176 restaurant within the castle walls. While the scene is idyllic, back in the day it was one of the frontline battle grounds between the Normans and the Welsh Princes. The castle changed hands several times.

1176 is a significant date. The castle was held by the Welsh under the leadership of The Lord Rhys ap Gruffydd. He organised the first Eisteddfod and it was held on this site in 1176. Lord Rhys must have felt safe and sure of his ground to arrange this spectacle, while no doubt breathing a sigh of relief when the Eisteddfod went off without violence. It must have been quite a show with competitors from all over Wales. We read that the peace and calm was retained because the men of the south won the singing contests and their rivals from the north won the bardic poetry event.

We walk down the hill to the Quay and across the bridge over the Teifi, turning right at a Fusion Asian restaurant. This is painted a startling yellow. It used to be the Eagle pub, where farmers would gather after a successful Monday selling their animals at Cardigan Mart.

Signposting is a little sketchy, but we eventually find the turn for St Dogmaels Abbey founded in the early twelfth century by the' Grey monks' as the only Tironian Order Abbey in England and Wales.

If you are lucky enough to visit on a Tuesday, the local produce market is worthy of a visit. The winner of a BBC Good Food Award, all the producers are located within a thirty mile radius.

We had a hearty lunch at the White Hart pub nearby.

Butterfly on thistle.

Mwnt to Llangrannog

It is August. There is a steady downpour, followed by a drenching. Our initial experience of the coast path has taught us to prepare for all weather. We are fully kitted out in our rain gear. It isn't the getting wet that is bothersome. It's the path turning into a muddy treacle mess.

The bracken is tall at this time of year and droops over the path in the rain. You can't see where to plant your feet. Lucy also spots a snake on this stretch, and with the summer adder warnings in place, we proceed with caution.

That said, this is a very pretty stretch of coastline, if you can ignore the conspicuous MOD security fence in Aberporth.

We walk north to south starting in Llangrannog and swiftly climb from the beachfront to the statue of St. Carannog. He founded the first church here somewhere between 480AD and 520AD. He was the grandson of Ceredig, of Ceredigion fame.

We touch the statue for luck and follow the cliff path, before heading through fields. With Pen y Bryn beach in our sights, the heavens open. We scurry onwards to the little tearoom called The Plwmp Tart, along with other crazy outdoor bikers and walkers.

The downpour soon stops, and we make our way into the small woodland across the car park. We clambered up some steep steps and were about to leave the woodland when it rained again! We stayed under the trees for some time before we headed for Tresaith, marvelling at a rainbow rising and falling into the sea.

The heathers are now adding colour to our journey; the Latin name for common heather is *Calluna Vulgaris* which sounds more like a nasty disease, not worthy of the purple carpet on the hillside.

The walk is a forager's dream, the hazelnut shells are hardening, the blackberries are ripening, the elder flowers have turned to berries and will soon be ready for that winter cold cure! So many rich pickings.

When walking, it is difficult to be definite about lunch stops, so we always have provisions and snacks. It is a bonus when we find a friendly establishment directly on our route. I don't need much persuading to divert into The Ship in Tresaith. We swap views for comfort and warmth, with a chance to take our rucksacks off and enjoy a tasty lunch rather than soggy sandwiches. Here in Tresaith, as in many of our food stops, the menu includes lots of local Welsh produce. The standard of service and quality of the food is first-class. It makes it quite difficult to restart!

Out into the damp air we go, crossing the beach, we look back and catch sight of the waterfall towards the far corner, before marching up the slope fortified by a 'good lunch' we are soon tackling the undulating path to Aberporth.

We pass a couple of converted railway carriages. I remember a cozy stay, a murder mystery weekend with friends in 'Wendy' one of the conversions.

Ceredigion's path signage may be a bit quirky, but we take our hats off to their public art. The Ship Skeleton Sculpture at the entrance to the beach at Aberporth catches our eye. Engraved in the stones are names of local ships that were lost at sea. A worthy homage to Aberporth's maritime heritage.

Crossing the beach, accessing the road past yet another Ship pub, we climb the seemingly never-ending Rhiw y Rofft, arriving breathless at the perimeter fence for the Ministry of Defence. Skirting around the outskirts, we follow the route across fields and woodland and over a series of footbridges.

At Pencestyll, we see warning signs for 'non-ionising radiation'. We are not sure what it means but we hurry through the kissing gates, passing the military installation on the hill towards our final stop Mwnt. The little white church nestling at the base of Foel y Mwnt is a sight for sore eyes.

The one thing about staying with family is the comfort of PJs, slippers and no pretence after a long day. While Lucy lingers in a hot bath, I shower and catch up with the family gossip. We enjoy a hearty supper, a convivial evening before heading to bed with a hot water bottle for our aching joints.

(above) Llangrannog.
(opposite, bottom) Lucy on the path from New Quay, testing how close the drop is.

New Quay and Llangrannog

The Ceredigion path seems to be gentler underfoot than its Pembrokeshire counterpart, but the ups and downs are just as punishing, particularly on a hot summer's day.

We explore New Quay and its Dylan Thomas connections. The debate still lingers whether the inspiration for *Under Milk Wood* and the town of Llaregub (try saying it backwards) came from New Quay or Laugharne. Probably a bit of both. We follow our nose up Rock Street to the Fish Factory and hit the first rise, and so it goes on.

Bird and dolphin watchers are out in force. Dolphins were spotted frolicking in New Quay harbour the previous night. Disappointingly, we don't spot any on our walk.

We stop at Melyn y Gors café in Cwmtydu for a morning coffee. As we came down the slope into the bay, there is a sign that says five and half miles to Llangrannog and the next sign, some three hundred yards along, says four and half miles to Llangrannog... confused or what?

The path goes alarmingly near the edge in parts. We meet a couple of people who say they hope we don't have vertigo and a little later, we can see their point. At one stage the track looks as if it heads over the cliff into the sea, a passing walker calls it 'The Path of Doom'.

Despite the edges, it's relatively easy to walk; a steady climb. We rest before we head up the slope towards Llangrannog Urdd Centre. Originally built in the 1930s for members of Urdd Gobaith Cymru, a youth movement for youngsters between the ages of eight to twenty-five to enjoy experiences through the medium of Welsh. It is a rite of passage for thousands of young Welsh speakers.

Further up the trail we run into Malcolm, who is walking and wild camping around Wales for two charities: Wales Air Ambulance and a deaf school in Ammanford.

He gives us a great overview of the difficulties we may face heading further north, while we share our experiences with the tides in Pembrokeshire and the challenges on the St Dogmaels to Newport stretch.

He is also a godsend when we reach Pendinas Lochtyn and meet him again. The signs seem to indicate an uphill climb, via a concrete path. He has just walked up to the top, as we are about to, but the path goes around Pendinas and curves away from Ynys Lochtyn towards Llangrannog.

He saves us much confusion as we would have been trying to find a direct route down the hill.

We soldier on to the pretty village of Llangrannog, grateful to have completed this stunning but deceptive section.

Llanon and New Quay

We have come a long way since the early days of walking the Wales Coast Path. Back then we vowed we wouldn't walk if it forecasted rain. While we still won't set out in the rain, if we get caught out by the weather we take it in our stride.

This is just as well, as it is a summer of sunshine and showers. We take a month off for various holiday commitments, and resume our walk in August, even though the forecast warns of changeable weather.

Five minutes into the walk, it pours down, but we persevere, donning our wet weather gear. This dries off quickly, but we are left steaming gently inside our jackets. It is so warm we are soon walking in shorts; our boots are theoretically waterproof.

This walk is not particularly challenging and is straightforward mainly along low cliffs.

Taking full advantage of our base with my family, we are once again heading south from Llanon, named after Non, the mother of St David, Patron Saint of Wales. The ground rises above Graig Ddu, and then a gentle descent into the pretty village of Aberarth. I had been told that Bath stone was imported by sea from Bristol and landed nearby for the building of Strata Florida Abbey.

We frequently reflect on how much more there is to these sleepy coastal villages than is apparent when driving through on the main road.

We stop for lunch at the Harbourmaster in Aberaeron, spending more time than we intend browsing through the shops. The harbour and the pastel painted Georgian houses make Aberaeron a charming place to stop on the Wales Coast Path. We spot some people we know but dodge out of sight. They are dressed to kill while we are in our weather-worn, slightly grubby walking gear.

We circle the harbour over the footbridge and pick up the path, through Gilfach yr Halen holiday village, eventually reaching Craig Ddu the only short steep climb on the walk.

A brief woodland walk near Cei Bach and then through a farmyard onto a road. At Pont Llanina, we check with a dog walker whether we were going to beat the tide to New Quay. At this point in the walk, we can take either the high or low tide option.

She figures, if we are pretty sharp we can walk across the beach, and if we aren't we can scramble across the rocks to the harbour at New Quay. We scramble across the rocks! The scramble is less than graceful. There are times during our experience when we think, 'why on earth?' This was one of them. Why on earth didn't we go the long way round? The answer to that is aching feet! A rather silly decision, not advisable in retrospect and potentially hazardous. We think we have enough time but don't take into account that we are tired at the end of the day, and the tide is moving faster than us. We scrape through. Looking back along the Bay we can see that the sea had reached the rocks. A narrow escape not to be repeated.

The last evening with my brother and his wife. They berate us good naturedly for taking chances. In the morning, Eileen presents us both with whistles in case we lose sight of each other on the path.

Llanon and Aberystwyth

Sometimes things happen when you walk. Leaving home on a Saturday morning, with the intention of walking constantly for three days, ends in a two-hour walk, and a stressed shoulder.

The morning starts with a pleasant encounter in the shared kitchen at Maes Bach, our self-service hotel in Aberystwyth. A young woman from Newfoundland offers to share her breakfast. She has been a student at the University of Aberystwyth and has taken Welsh lessons. She is on her way to Nant Gwrtheyrn for a Welsh refresher course. She loves Wales.

We speak in Welsh. She tells us she is currently living in Denmark and learning Danish. We admire her youthful commitment to absorbing the language and culture of both countries.

I am experiencing a few twinges as we set off across the university town of Aberystwyth, over the bridge across the River Rheidol, skirting Tanybwlch beach, with a view across at Pendinas and the monument commemorating the Duke of Wellington and Waterloo.

Following a steep climb up Allt Wen, we trudge along to Morfa Bychan, where I give in to the pain. Every movement of my shoulder is torture. I am in agony. The lovely team at the caravan park call a taxi back to the guest house. Pain killers and an early night are in order.

A sleepless night doesn't help matters. It is best to call it a day, but not before I had 'Kicked the Bar'. It is a strange local tradition, but it is meant to bring good luck. I feel I need it for the drive home. Lucy comes into her own, negotiating our cancelled booking with the owners, who are very obliging given our circumstances. We then walk towards Constitution Hill and locate the Bar. We kicked it hard and then take in the Sunday food market on our way back. The quality of the local food on display looked appetising. A few purchases made and I am grateful to be on my way home.

A lesson learned – I not only need good legs for walking, I also need the rest of my body to be fully functioning.

August Bank Holiday and we are in the brilliant sunshine after a month of showers. We complete the walk, curtailed due to my now diagnosed rotor cuff problems. This time we head north from the little village of Llanon.

Friendly villagers help us on our way by showing us a shortcut down to the sea between the houses. We are soon making our way past St Bride's Church in Llansantffraed and make good time on the two and half mile walk to Llanrhystud, passing several lime kilns on the way.

We walk up the lane towards the village, and double back on ourselves through Pengarreg Caravan Park. We stop here to enjoy a cool drink and take in the bank holiday car boot sale. The water colour I fancy is a bit too large to carry for the next few miles. We don't stay for the advertised Sumo wrestling entertainment!

Once past the caravan park, the path is wonderfully isolated. We only see one other group of walkers, although our peace is initially shattered by the sound of what we call 'motorised sea chariots' out on the bay – it is a bank holiday after all!

(above) A sign of autumn.
(opposite) A smiling buoy.

When the noise stops, we walk in perfect silence for miles, the only distraction is a red kite swooping down towards the sea, and some curious sheep. We call this the mushroom walk, based on the number of fungi we come across. As a child I used to think of them as fairy (*tylwyth teg*) houses.

The path itself has worn into a single file groove. We look like a pair of drunks walking home from the pub, with one foot in the ditch and one on the road.

We stop at Penderi Cliffs to watch a pregnant cow seal sunbathing on the rocks below. Great excitement as this is only the second seal we have seen on our walk along the coast.

There are a couple of farms along this stretch, and they look so in keeping with the landscape – solitary and sturdy. The trees that surround them are stunted and bent by the winds. Some of the coastal fencing has been moved further inland to account for an eroding coastline.

Judging from a rusty gate, and one hanging on a hinge, it doesn't appear that many people have walked this way. The ease of the walk, and the peace and quiet is very satisfying.

We stay at Penrhos Golf Club, the only one-night stay booking available for the bank holiday weekend. We are delighted with it: large rooms, good Wi-Fi, etc. We sink a glass or two of wine, and savour a perfectly cooked steak, served by a charming bespectacled young man and a lovely raspberry haired young woman, both of whom are extremely helpful.

Tre Taliesin to Aberystwyth

Tre Taliesin is a small village with limited parking. We find a lay-by on the outskirts: The Machynlleth side.

Taliesin was a bardic poet from the sixth century. Frank Lloyd Wright, a renowned architect named his home in America, Taliesin after the poet, but with a nod to his grandparents who emigrated from Ceredigion to America. Wright's style of architecture creates harmony between people and nature.

Good signposting down Church Street and for about four miles the walk is straightforward. Through Cors Fochno, also known as Borth Bog, part of the Dyfi National Nature reserve, a designated UNESCO Biosphere site.

The reserve is a vast area of wetlands. We are joined on our walk through the bog by a large heron, which swoops up from the ditches as we approach, leading the way through the peat mire. Its broad wingspan reminds Lucy of a pterodactyl.

The horse flies are not such welcome companions, multiple itchy bites from the persistent beggars!

Onwards to Borth, where people are very friendly, telling us all about the submerged forest and pointing us to a sculpture in Welsh slate inspired by the forest and the Legend of Cantre'r Gwaelod. This ancient legend speaks of a fabulous city covering the length of Cardigan Bay which was drowned by the incoming sea.

We stop for a cuppa at Oriel Tir a Mor, yet another welcoming venue. They cater for small walking groups, so worthy of noting.

We make our way through the sleepy town, heading up the slope to the war memorial. Looking down at Borth, it looks very vulnerable. The view takes in the curve of Cardigan Bay, across Dovey Estuary to the Llŷn and Snowdon peak.

The leisurely start to this leg has lulled us into thinking the walk is going to be super easy. Not so, from the monument to Clarach Bay the path rises and falls constantly.

Thankfully, it evens out somewhat for the last stretch to Constitution Hill, where we are rewarded by a magnificent panoramic view of Aberystwyth, and south to Cardigan Bay.

Taking a breather, we gratefully zig-zag our way down alongside the Cliff Railway to the Promenade below.

I am convinced that had the funicular railway been running, we would have taken the ride down to Aberystwyth; not only to save our aching bodies, but to experience the joy of travelling on the longest railway of its kind in Britain.

Aberystwyth is strangely quiet as we go in search of a bite to eat. It is too early for the restaurants to open, but too late for the cafés. The students have not made it back to the university yet from their summer break. They are the lifeblood of this town; without them it is strangely haunting.

We find a Middle Eastern restaurant about to open and dive in.

Machynlleth and Tre Taliensin

" *I would walk five hundred miles and I would walk five hundred more…"* hat was the song of the day, sung originally by the Proclaimers, but today by two happy ladies. Our goal was to complete the Ceredigion stage of the Wales Coast Path and reach the five hundred milestone.

This walk does not go anywhere near the coast, crossing the Dyfi estuary. It takes you well inland, through back lanes, coniferous forest and ancient woodlands, with some first-class views over the Dyfi estuary.

We are a bit apprehensive setting off. We have been warned that the route is not clearly signposted, and we have forgotten our map book!

Our fears are misplaced. There are only two places where we are slightly unsure, otherwise clear signposting with white top posts guided us clearly through large fields.

A note of caution here – for anyone planning to rendezvous in Mid Wales, allow for the possibility of little or no telephone signal. Lucy was unavoidably delayed. I was in Machynlleth bright and early, and a lengthy wait ensued. This is the first time there had been any confusion, but no harm done.

To while away the time, I walk into Machynlleth. The town was waking, ready for its weekly market. I turn right at the Clock Tower and stroll until I reach the sixteenth century building Canolfan Owain Glyndŵr. In 1404, on this site

Owain had set up a Welsh Parliament, in direct conflict with King Henry IV.

Catching up with Lucy in the car park at Plas Machynlleth, we waste no time in setting off, picking up the signs for both Glyndwr Way and the Wales Coast Path' which run parallel at this stage. Up the well-trodden 'Roman Steps', the first of our many ascents on this walk.

There are numerous twists and turns on this route…

We diverge from Glyndwr Way down a leafy lane, through a field, onto a road towards Garthgwynion, continuing through the woodland of Llyfnant Valley.

We pass a house called Felin Llyfnant onto a road, cross a bridge, and then take a left at a junction. We now cross from Meirionnydd into Ceredigion – just a short hop to completing the Ceredigion path.

At a cluster of buildings, we reach the aptly named Caerhedyn, field of bracken. There is good dual use of bridleways for walking and riding along this stretch. We thankfully skirt Craig Caerhedyn and start getting tantalising glimpses of the Dyfi estuary in the distance, before being exposed to the full view down towards Aberdovey and across to Ynys Las and Borth.

Dry stone walls, horses grazing on Foel Fawr, the bracken covered hillside turning brown as autumn approaches. We go onwards towards Cwm Einon, otherwise known as Artists Valley, so called after the nineteenth century artists who made their way here.

Members of Led Zeppelin lived in Bron yr Aur, a farmhouse in Artists Valley and they completed *Led Zeppelin 111* here. They may have started writing '*Stairway to Heaven*' here, although this is open to debate. A line from the song comes to mind 'In the tree by the brook, there's a songbird who sings'. The water tumbles crystal clear, the moss is a deep green. The air is so clean, fine filaments of lichen hang from the trees. They could have been standing right here when inspiration struck. I am living the moment.

From Cwm Einon there is road and track, we meander through several fields neatly guided by white topped signposts, before heading down to the main road at Tre'r Ddol then through the village to Tre Taliesin.

Finally, we are over the five hundred mile target. Ceredigion path completed.

Aberdyfi to Machynlleth

A grey dawn, turning to rain. With our wet weather gear on, we head out of Aberdyfi passing the Literary Institute on the right, turning sharply uphill to the left where it says *Araf*/Slow on the road. The climb and steps are quite steep, but the views over the town and harbour are worth the breathless effort.

Leaving Aberdyfi behind, we bear right onto the quarry road, and before you know it, you are heading left up the gorse covered Cefn Rhos, passing a stream heading uphill.

It has been raining heavily and the fields are mucky mires. The cattle stare down at us from their vantage point on the hill, probably wondering what on earth we are doing there in such weather!

Going through a gate to the left of the farmyard and barn, we are now making good time along the road above Cwm Maethlon, Happy Valley. The rain has turned to a steady drizzle, but well worth pausing to enjoy the view.

We reach the slate marker for Carn March Arthur. Legend has it that Llamrai, King Arthur's horse, left a hoof print while dragging the monster Afanc out of the nearby lake.

The tracks across the moors become quite rutted and filled with water. To avoid getting wet over our boots we steer off the path, only to find it harder to cross the boggy terrain. This is Lucy's first baptism by Bog, which necessitates a change of clothing when we get to firmer ground.

The signposting has been great. An easy walk passing a felled forest wood, eventually reaching the main road, and crossing over to Cefn Crib caravan park.

This is where it all goes horribly wrong. A car is parked in a gateway, but little do we know that behind this car is a low-lying sign for the coast path. We miss it and continue down a track. With no other sign in sight, we follow the green and yellow signs through mud and bog. We arrive at a wooden bridge that has been blocked off because it is rotten. We can see the road across the field, so we just have to carry on.

It is a field like no other, a genuine 'sink if you stand still' bog. Lucy is standing still and slowly sinking.

'Launch yourself at the reeds,' I shout. She looks at me in horror and dramatically hurls herself across the bog, ending in a half crouch. Grabbing hold of the reeds she steadies herself, reverting to standing position, then propels herself forward to sink once again into the bog. Shouting encouragement while I skirt around the boggy bits, I am getting a tad worried as the sinking episode recurs four or five times as Lucy valiantly throws herself at first one clump of reeds then another. Lucy is a self-confessed townie – nervous and maybe slightly hysterical when confronted with animals and other countryside dangers. She is in a right old state by the time we stagger across the field and clamber over a wall onto the road like two muddy rats.

We are so grateful to Deilwen at Gogarth Hall Farm holidays. The lady there takes pity on us, makes us a cup of tea and calls us a taxi. It helps that she knew our ex-boss. Thank the Lord for kind people.

The taxi driver is totally unfazed by two wet, muddy females falling into her cab.

In the past I might have over emphasised my own upbringing as a country girl, and faked a confidence, that I sometimes lacked, to stave off any hysteria which might make the situation worse. I have led Lucy through fields of cows and sheep, past dogs, and across rivers with stepping stones; walking without hesitation while aware of the slight whimpering behind me or a hand reaching out to grab my backpack. I might have looked as if I knew what I was doing, but it wasn't always the case. I was seriously shaken by the bog experience and would certainly have been terrified if I had thrown myself face first into it multiple times. Growing up on the Preseli Hills, we were warned not to go near the boggy area, y Pwll y Gwydd or any marshland for that matter. Horse and carts had been sunk were the dire warnings. Pwll y Gwydd was 'bottomless'.

I let Lucy believe we were not in any real danger as she continues to talk and re-enact the bog dance while demolishing a bottle of wine.

I feel only a slight twinge of guilt as Lucy praises my countryside savvy, knowing that I would have had a real tantrum if I had fallen into that quagmire.

Obviously, we didn't reach Machynlleth that day. Thoroughly tired out we make for our beds knowing we will be dining out on the experience for months, if not years to come. Thus Bog-gate becomes part of the slow walking legend.

Next day, the dawn is bright and beautiful. To complete the walk, we decide to head from Machynlleth towards Cefn Crib Caravan Park, where we went horribly wrong the previous day.

Enjoying the sunshine, we pass the gothic clock tower, across Dovey Bridge, turning left and then a right, up a lane unsuitable for heavy vehicles. It is a steep climb, but the autumn colours and the view from the top are well worth the effort.

Right turn off the lane and the climb continues to the crest of the hill, then down through a forest path until we reach a forestry road. Turning left, we are glad of the shade of the forest to cool us down, as it is getting a little bit warm climbing up the hill.

This walk is well signposted. We stop at Pennal. This is where the Welsh Prince, Owain Glyndŵr held his final senate meeting. Owain Glyndŵr sent a letter to Charles VI of France in 1406 looking for support for an independent Wales and his rebellion from English Rule. These Pennal letters today are held in the Archives Nationales de France in Paris. Can we have them back please? They mean so much to us.

The church of St Peter ad Vincula, Pennal was founded in the sixth century, much of today's church dates to the eighteenth century.

Pennal is one of twenty-one locations known for the courts of the Princes of Gwynedd, and the memorial garden is dedicated to the memory of native Welsh Princes. A statue of Owain Glyndŵr takes pride of place. It is a place for quiet reflection, a small village with a huge history.

As we depart, we note the gravestones artfully displayed around the memorial garden providing insights into the more recent social history of the area.

Not wanting another encounter with the 'Bog', we walk along the road to Cefn Crib.

(opposite) Owain Glyndŵr's statue in Pennal.

OWAIN GLYN DŴR
Coronwyd yn Dywysog Cymru
16 Medi 1404
Machynlleth
"invicta virtus, vultus integer"
RW
Cerflunydd
Dave Haynes
dadorchuddiwyd
4 Medi 2004

Rhoslefain to Aberdyfi

We are now getting Wales Coast Path withdrawal symptoms after a gap in our schedule. It is two months since our 'Bog-gate' experience.

The walk took us from Rhoslefain to Aberdyfi. Storm Brian hasn't quite finished blowing itself out, so we are holed up in the pretty harbour town of Aberdovey, or Aberdyfi, as the Welsh spelling goes. No great hardship, a bit of retail therapy, lots of places to eat and drink, and our wee flat is right on the harbour.

Eventually the rain clears, and we head out with glee. We can hear a haunting bell far offshore, and we talk about the Bells of Aberdyfi. In the legend, Seithenyn was supposed to have closed the sluice gates of the dyke protecting Cantre'r Gwaelod. He got drunk one night and forgot to do it; the area was drowned but the bells can still be heard tolling under the sea.

Leaving our car in a farm lane in Rhoslefain, we are careful not to cause any obstruction. We are particularly mindful that locals need to get on with their days work without cars barring their way. We follow the track, then field to field, aiming for a large White House in the distance. Then onto the road at Bwlch (there are loads of places called *Bwlch* in Wales. It means a pass). Sat Navs have been known to get confused.

It is a brilliant day for walking. The air is clear and everything looks newly washed and laundered after the storm.

Reaching the cycle path across the *Afon*/River Dysynni, the walk to Tywyn is straightforward. The caravans along the front soon come into sight, with lots of dog walkers about who look glad to be strolling in the sunshine. Their dogs are bundles of energy. Lucy is not fond of dogs and tries to detour around them.

At the end of the lengthy promenade in Tywyn, we eventually reach the sand dunes and take an easy walk, passing Aberdyfi golf course (one of the best links courses in Wales). Dropping down to the pebble foreshore, the tide is out. Instead we're able to make our way across the pebbles onto the long sandy beach all the way to Aberdyfi, skirting the yacht club to reach our apartment located over Nandora's dress shop.

Dinner at Coast Deli is the end of a perfect day's walking.

Llwyngwril remembrance.

Llwyngwril to Rhoslefain

A short walk of around six kilometres, one of our top and tail walks, just long enough to stretch our legs after a three-hour drive.

Llwyngwril is a village of some five hundred people, but it deserves to take centre stage for this walk. The yarn bombers of Llwyngwril have been busy over the past couple of years. Some people paint the town, but the good folk of Llwyngwril have decided to knit the town.

Numerous mice and rats adorn the bridge. Blodeuwedd, a heroine from the Mabinogi, stands proud on a green space in front of some houses. As we turn up a side road by the church, the war memorial has a large display of knitted poppies.

There is quite a steep walk up the hill onto a common, over a couple of cattle grids, and right onto a farm lane. Stiles and ladders are the order of the day.

The walk is well signposted, with atmospheric stone walls, patchwork fields and the picturesque ruin of an old cottage.

Despite the steep terrain, it doesn't take long before we descend towards the main road at Rhoslefain. It is a bit muddy in parts, mainly due to recent rain.

Standing stones.

Llwyngwril to Barmouth

We take the early train out of Barmouth to Llwyngwril. We are joined on our walk for this stretch by our friend, Louise Tambini, who is a passionate advocate for Keep Wales Tidy, and adds a little pace and energy to our efforts.

If you've never taken the journey on the Cambrian Coast Railway, you should give it a go. It must be the most scenic coastal train journey in the whole of the UK.

The conductor says that we will enjoy our walk as it 'is truly beautiful, with a few ups and downs, but marvellous views'. She is right on all counts.

It is a joy to be back in Llwyngwril. We notice more of the village yarn bombing masterpieces as we walk from the station. It puts a smile on our faces. The sun is shining, and all is well with the world.

We turn off the main road at Garthangharad Hotel. It is quite a steep climb from the village and out on the moorland. We are now close to one thousand feet above sea level, with views out to the Mawddach. Standing stones, old ruins, ancient settlements set against the burnished autumn bracken, makes this a very atmospheric walk.

The walk is quite straightforward until we get to Cyfannedd. We loop around a farmhouse; a homemade mileage marker has been placed against a stone seating area. Ahead we are confronted with a confusion of signs,

Lucy and Louise.

none of them clearly indicating our route. Someone has sprayed an arrow in red paint and, luckily, we opt for this. We head over a small stream and downhill through a bed of bracken and woodland.

Nearing Friog we make a slight detour to see the Blue Lake in a disused quarry. I believe that the site will soon be closed by the owner due to the rubbish left by visitors. We are fortunate.

Barmouth is to the north, but a sign points south. Trusting the sign, we shortly turn off towards Fairbourne, where we encounter a lady emerging from the beach wrapped in a towel, and wearing Doc Martens. This is not what you expect in November.

I feel for the residents of Fairbourne, as the town is designated for managed retreat because of the rising sea levels.

The so-called Dragon's Teeth dominate the front in Fairbourne. They are tank traps dating back to World War II. Crossing the narrow-gauge railway, we make short work of crossing towards Morfa Mawddach.

Views of the Mawddach estuary sustain us as we walk up the wooden bridge attached to the railway bridge and into Barmouth.

Surprised by alpacas.

Llanenddwyn to Barmouth

It is a very rainy Sunday morning. We defer our walk until mid-morning, as it's a short walk before our drive home. In watery sunshine we walk up the road from Llanenddwyn, and head towards Bennar-Fawr. The walk is straightforward, if a tad fragmented, through field, caravan and camping parks. We follow a long stretch along the main A496 (some two miles), before turning off towards the beach at Barmouth.

It is worth looking inland towards Egryn, the National Trust land with its complex network of stone walling. It is a true rural craft that has stood the test of time, with not a trowel of cement in sight.

I pause to take photographs and I hear a yell from Lucy. She has been surprised by alpacas coming through the gap in the wall. We are well-used to sheep, but alpacas are a first!

A lengthy walk along the Promenade, the groynes casting long shadows on the sand.

We are rewarded with a rainbow at the end of our walking weekend. Is there a crock of gold?

Back in our little house next to The Last Inn pub, we pick up the car and head for the NorBar for a well-earned late Sunday lunch, before the journey south and home.

(above) Harlech Castle.
(opposite) Rainbow on the Mawddach.

Harlech to Llanenddwyn

Harlech is simply dominated by Harlech Castle, towering forbiddingly on a rocky crag. It is one of Edward I's most imposing sites of oppression. Owain Glyndŵr held it in 1404 and used it as his stronghold for a short while. It is not our focus today as we head for the beach, away from the town passing Royal St David's Golf Course.

Harlech Beach, with four miles of golden sand, is a great start to the day. Louise is so full of the joys of walking. She turns cartwheels on the beach. Steep steps lead up from the beach, across the railway line and beyond, one hundred and twelve in total. The path leads onto the main road for a few hundred yards before turning right towards the coastal settlement of Llandanwg, a place I had never visited before.

We stop at the Beach café and get to know a fat robin. We chat to the café owner who is extremely passionate about the events planned for the 'Year of the Sea'. He also notices we are wearing plastic bags between our socks and boots! Our boots are very damp from previous days and we are resorting to emergency measures. He warns us of the danger of 'Trench Foot'!

I stroll across to the tiny medieval church of St Tanwg, known locally as the church in the sand. It dates back to the thirteenth century, with some references to sixth century. Much of the graveyard is covered in dunes, but some of the gravestones have been rescued and date from the fifteenth century.

We walk across the salt marshes, and along the Artro estuary passing the little harbour and eventually reaching a level crossing. Workmen are in action, so we follow the path south, and then right to a very smart footbridge crossing the river.

From Llanbedr we take the road to Shell Island passing through Llanbedr airfield. We reach a concrete walkway across the reed beds, skirting the SSSI dunes of Morfa Dyffryn, a habitat for wading birds. There is a concrete path leading through the dunes and are surrounded by dancing reeds as far as the eye could see. It is quite unnerving as we follow the raised yellow walkway. Lucy revels in the landscape and we enter into a chorus of *Follow the Yellow Brick Road.*

This leads us onto the longest stretch of unspoiled beach, deserted apart from us and a couple of jellyfish. We jokingly deliberate if we should have to take our clothes off, should we be confronted by irate naturists on the designated beach area, but today nobody is brave enough to expose all to the nippy November air.

We seem to have walked miles along the beach and we are beginning to think we might have missed the white and red marker post to lead us to the boardwalk and into the car parking area in Llanenddwyn. It is not long before our tracker Lucy spots the marker. Another day and this coast of Wales just keeps on giving.

Harlech beach.

Farm ruin near the Dwyryd estuary.

Penrhyndeudraeth to Harlech

One of these days, we may return to walk the old route for the Wales Coast Path. The old path heads inland to Maentwrog before coming back towards Llandecwyn. The new Pont Briwet Bridge has shortened the route considerably.

The route is well signposted. The only minor confusion is just after scrambling up and around the low hill at Bryn Glas, it is difficult to locate the style to cross over the railway. A very messy farm track also needs negotiating. Crossing a dyke, the water levels below are swollen with the rains of recent days. It isn't surprising, given the rainfall, that the path is really muddy, which makes it quite slithery and slippy.

It is winter walking after all!

On a beautiful stretch along the salt marsh, we feel a bit guilty discussing the merit of salt marsh lamb while looking out at the sheep!

Reaching the road at Ynys and following the route we reach the atmospheric Llanfihangel y Traethau church / St Michael's of the Sands. I am saddened by one gravestone, a lady called Gwen who died at forty-eight and was buried with two daughters in their teens. Mari y Fantell Wen (Mary of the white cloak or simply Mary Evans) who thought she was the bride of

The Italianate village, Portmeirion.

Christ, is also buried in the churchyard. Not everybody shares my love of graveyards, so it was time to move on.

Over the bracken covered moor, we reach the estuary and enjoy stunning views of the Italianate village of Portmeirion and Porthmadog beyond.

The only blot on the landscape of this walk is the landfill site at Morfa Harlech, but we hurry along towards Harlech as we are losing daylight.

We are not worried about the fading light as we can see that we are fast approaching Harlech. The castle is an ominous but welcoming shadow on the hill.

Samson's Bay near Borth y Gest.

Llŷn Peninsula 112.75 miles – 181.5kms
Gorau Prinder – Prinder Geiriau – The Best Scarcity is the Scarcity of Words.

Penrhyndeudraeth, Porthmadog and Criccieth

Sunday morning and a glorious dawn full of flame-coloured skies, crisp and cold. This turns out to be a fantastic, picturesque walk. We complete this walk in two bursts, Penrhyndeudraeth to Porthmadog followed by a bus trip to Criccieth and walk back to Porthmadog.

This is mainly because it is only three degrees centigrade at dawn, and the thought that we may need a warming break during the day. We are staying in a harbourside apartment in Porthmadog, which was mid-point on our walk, so we decide to pop home and have some lunch. We reframe our route by taking the bus to Criccieth so we will end the walk at our apartment.

From Penrhyndeudraeth the walk skirts Portmeirion and it is too early to divert for a coffee. We have driven along the Cob in Porthmadog many times but not walked its length. Lucy and I couldn't have picked a better day. The mountains are clearly reflected in the water, wading birds are out in force, looking for their breakfast no doubt. Very few cars at such an early hour – an exquisite stillness!

Fast forward to Criccieth, a stop for coffee at Tir a Mor, a popular stop for *Sunday Times* readers, with every other table engrossed in the papers. Not a bad way to start the day.

On the beach, there is a birthday group, some in the water swimming. It is getting warmer!

We walk away from Criccieth Castle, which dominates the town. The castle was initially built by Llywelyn the Great and added to by his grandson Llywelyn the Last. It then became an Edward I bastion in the thirteenth century. The castle was used as a prison until 1404, when it was seized by Owain Glyndŵr's forces and walls were torn down and then set alight.

Walking towards the north of Wales we come across the victories and defeats of the family Llewelyn and of Owain Glyndŵr, and the conflict between Wales and the various corresponding Kings of England.

We stop to take in the view across the bay to the castle. It isn't surprising that Turner found it a suitable subject to paint, as Criccieth Castle stands out proudly on the hill. While pausing, we are approached by two ladies, who ask if we are walking the Wales Coast Path. They are from Mwnt and are also on a walking mission and are enjoying the experience as much as we are.

The early stage of the walk is mainly on low ground, with a slight rise to Black Rock. There is a lengthy walk along Black Rock Sands, which isn't black. A speed limit is in place for the cars on the beach. Some boy racers are doing their best to ignore the signs. We splash through the streams running down to the sea at Morfa Bychan. The November tides have washed up a number of alien looking jellyfish. Strange looking creatures – do they serve a purpose?

A little scramble off the beach at Ynys Cyngar, and a well-placed seat for our water break, before taking in the broadwalk towards Samson's Bay, eventually reaching steps and a bit of a steep walk through the woods.

We are always grateful for seats dotted around the coast, in memory of the dearly departed, they too must have enjoyed the views.

It is plain sailing to the pretty harbour at Borth y Gest, and onwards to Porthmadog.

Whether it is the November sunshine or the magic of the Llŷn Peninsula, this is a truly memorable walk.

Changing out of our walking clothes we have enough energy left to explore Porthmadog, reminding ourselves that Welsh slate that roofed the world was exported from here. No trace of that busy period now, just a pretty marina with the Ffestiniog and Highland Welsh Railway reflecting two hundred years of history.

We relish the independent shops that are doing a busy trade on this cold day. We end the day with a short drive to Caernarfon, dinner at the Black Boy and National Theatre Live *The Follies* at the Galeri. A bit of light entertainment is well worth the early start to the walk.

Criccieth Castle.

Criccieth and Pwllheli

I get out of bed feeling cranky '*llwyr fy mhenol*' as we say in Welsh and a good literal translation would be 'dragging my backside'. At 3.00am the rain is lashing against the bedroom window. It is very murky in the pre-dawn.

We drive to Criccieth in silence. Lucy is as enthusiastic about the forthcoming walk as I am. It gets you like that sometimes. Will it be lashing rain? Shall we put it off until tomorrow?

I think it was C S Lewis who said, 'Walking and talking are two great pleasures, but it is a shame to combine them both'. We had walked in companionable silence for miles lost in thought, but today was the silence of two grumpy women, not to be broken.

Criccieth looks dark and forbidding this morning as the waves lash against the beach front. Hard to believe that people were swimming in the sea the previous day.

Donning our wet weather gear, I frequently opt for wellies instead of boots in wet weather, worn with a pair of cashmere bed socks, I rarely suffer from blisters, while Lucy opts to carry a pair of dry socks and boots in her backpack, so at least one change is possible.

We set off up the hill with the castle to our left, along the promenade with the B&B and hotels on our right. The signposting has been great, if occasionally discreet, during these few last stages of our walk.

We are walking very quickly on a path beside a field, the waves crashing below, rather glad we are on a raised path.

We welcome the duckboards along Afon Dwyfor. The river is running high, and ducks and wild geese are crowded on a small island in the centre. Our mood lifts; it's not a bad day after all. The winter sun is trying to make an appearance.

Over a railway bridge, and down a lane past a farm, and then onto the main road. After half a mile I am grumpy again! The traffic noise is intrusive, and we have passed Llanystumdwy, wishing we had made a detour to the village to see the childhood home and burial place of David Lloyd George, leader of the Liberals, and who to date has served as the only ever Welsh Prime Minister. Between 1916 to 1922 he led Britain through World War I and introduced National Insurance amongst other things. A diversion would have broken the monotony of this stretch.

Our conversation centres around the difficulty of designing a coast path, the need to cross rivers, accommodate landowners, terrain, etc. We become more charitable about the need to take in the A497, but we are glad to turn off at Afon Wen.

A chocolate labrador pup, with a very deep bark, bounds up to us as we reach the railway bridge, a leaping four legged lovely who would win any heart.

I am delighted with my choice of footwear as the path leading to Hafan y Mor is a bit mucky. The large caravan park (used to be Butlins until 1987, now owned by Haven) is not very intrusive as seen from the coast.

Around Pen y Chain we go, the only rise in a very flat walk, down and across a very long beach Morfa Abererch; a combination of sand dune, pebbles and sand walking. This beach leads us to Pwllheli, passing the fine harbour development and around the promenade of the inner harbour straight to Pwllheli railway station.

We take a very neat trip on the Cambrian railway back to Criccieth to pick up the car, sharing our journey with a group of happy lady shoppers.

All in all, not the most inspiring, mainly due to the stretch along the main road and the threat of rain, but both of us very satisfied that we have completed yet another eleven miles along the Wales Coast Path.

Flooded broadwalk at Dwyfor Estuary.

Llanbedrog beach huts.

Llanbedrog to Pwllheli

With winter walking you need to study the weather forecast closer than you would for a wedding! We figure we can manage some five miles, before the predicted high winds and rain after lunch.

The threat of adverse weather doesn't stop us from walking around the gallery shops in Pwllheli. Lucy is on the hunt for a picture which represents our journey and the Wales Coast Path. I sneak into Elspeth Mills my favourite dress shop in this part of the world and come out clutching a bright red winter coat. We stop off at the local Spar to pick up our provisions for dinner and next day's picnic. This must be the best corner shop in Wales, with a wide range of wines, juice bar, sea food and a live lobster tank! We put it down to sophisticated locals and the needs of the Mancunian and Wirral set heading to Abersoch.

The inner-shopper satisfied we made for Llanbedrog beach, starting the walk from the National Trust car park. The colourful beach huts add a bit of cheer to an otherwise gloomy day.

Never having been to Llanbedrog in the winter, it is strange to see the beach devoid of people, as it is teeming in the summer months. We walk along the beach then up some steps into a field. We elect to drop down onto

Pwllheli.

the beach after Carreg y Defaid, while the coast path sticks to the fields above. We realise why when we reach the sea defences and scramble upwards to rejoin the path as it runs alongside the golf course.

From the Promenade it is a short walk into Pwllheli town centre, picking up a few more Christmas gifts at Tonnau gallery, before heading to Dylan's restaurant in Criccieth for an exceedingly long and enjoyable lunch.

It starts to rain as we were make our way to the restaurant. The weather forecast had been spot on. We don't care. We still love the Llŷn, but it was almost time to go home. Until the next time...

Abersoch.

Machroes to Llanbedrog

A straightforward route. We elect to stay on the beach until Abersoch, then through the village to the junction at the Londis stores, passing the harbour with its colourful boats and buoys. We head up the hill on the Pwllheli road, before taking one of the paths back down to the beach.

We are blessed with golden December sunshine, turning to amber in the late afternoon.

We walk along the beach passing The Warren, probably one of the most expensive and exclusive chalet parks in Wales. One chalet is known to have been bought for half a million pounds sterling!

We are grateful for the easy stroll across the sand, before turning off up a sandy path and following the signs up the forbidding Mynydd Tir-y-Cwmwd – The Headland. Our reward after a steep climb is the great view back across the bay.

Overall, the rocky headland is a comfortable walk, considering the time of year. The bare rocks are a help not a hindrance.

Around the headland, before the steep steps down, is the outlook down to the beach at Llanbedrog and across to Pwllheli. It is now dusk and the sky turns pink and the moon appears.

Lucy draws my attention to the Tin Man, the sculpture is a replacement for the original wooden man – a ship's figurehead.

Then comes the steep descent down the steps to Plas Glyn y Weddw. We are just in time to pop in and see the latest art exhibition and browse in the gallery and shop.

Heading back into Abersoch, we are joined by our guest weekend walker Louise Tambini.

One of the nicest things about our walking exploits is joining in with whatever is happening in the area. We are lucky enough to join in with the Abersoch Christmas festivities. My friend Jane is away, but we catch up with her husband John marshalling the activities. Her son Jack is a great host, offering us champagne in one of the local shops. He gets a result as we all make purchases.

It is great fun seeing Father Christmas arrive by fire engine, watched by excited kids and parents. Most of the shops are open late offering bubbly and chocolate. They live large in Abersoch.

Tin Man of Llanbedrog.

St Hywyn's Church, Aberdaron.

Llangenen to Machroes

The day starts with some very frisky cattle being moved along the road to new pasture. It looks as if the whole farming family is out in force to help with the operation.

We park up in the Sun Inn car park in Llanengan, before making our way through the fields to Pentowyn, climbing up the cliff to follow the waymarked route.

Reading up on local history, we find that lead was mined in the area, and the Tan Rallt lead mine is testament to the industrial history of the late nineteenth century.

Once we access the route, we find it to be plain sailing.

The walk is varied, common land of Mynydd Cilan, around Trwyn Cian and Trwyn Llech y Ddol (*Trwyn* is Welsh for nose – not surprisingly as we are at the tip of this Peninsula).

The heather and gorse are rather dull in the winter light, but would add a glorious hue when in bloom. The rust-coloured bracken adds depth and richness to the winter landscape.

There is an easy grassy stretch across the cliffs overlooking Porth Ceiriad, following the curve of this picturesque beach to reach Trwyn yr Wylfa. The

We will always find a sheep on our walk.

highlight of the walk is around Penrhyn Ddu, with the offshore St Tudwal's Islands catching our eye at every turn. St Tudwal was a Breton monk who became a hermit on one of the islands in the sixth century. The adventurer Bear Grylls now has a home on one of the islands.

We follow a stony road down to Machroes. The road itself is closed and in a bad state of repair.

Reaching the car park, we drive around to Llanengan, where we parked the other car and have a pleasant lunch at the Sun Inn while watching the Wales v South Africa rugby match. Rubbish game despite a Wales win.

Sunset at Porth Neigwl.

Llangenen and Aberdaron

Depending on which mileage chart you read, this walk is either twelve miles, twelve and half miles, or according to Louise's fitness tracker we have walked fourteen miles. The only certainty is that it is the muckiest winter walk since starting on the Wales Coast Path.

An early morning drive from Abersoch to Aberdaron certainly makes us appreciate the remoteness of this part of the Llŷn, and also its raw beauty.

The first thing that strikes you in Aberdaron is the church overlooking the beach. St Hywyn's Church, Aberdaron dates from the twelfth century, but stems from a much earlier period – some say from the fifth century. When Bardsey Island and St Davids were designated pilgrim sites by the Pope in the late twelfth century, the church came into its own. Feeding a multitude of pilgrims and offering sanctuary. I find the setting and the solid grey structure of the church bleak yet comforting. R S Thomas, the esteemed Welsh poet was a vicar here from 1967 to 1978.

The remote rather cranky poet must have felt a kinship with this equally remote church by the sea.

Aberdaron itself is a small windswept seaside village, with mainly white-washed houses. It would have been the last rest stop before pilgrims crossed over to Bardsey Island, the burial island of twenty thousand saints. National Trust's Porth y Swnt meaning Gateway to the Sound is an excellent interpretation centre for human history and nature of the Llŷn, with a handy café. We take advantage of the car park and facilities.

We debate outside the local shop as to which direction to take, our guidebook soon puts us right; we turn into a field and we are on our way.

The path as far as Porth Yago is well-defined if somewhat wet. The industrial ruins add to the atmosphere. The lane leading up to a guest house is covered with deep mud, and the electric fence running alongside seems forbidding. It is after the iron gate leading out of the farmyard that the confusion begins. The book says turn left, the signs mark the route as straight on, and with one sign pointing randomly towards the heath.

We go straight on and come to a superb viewpoint looking out on Bardsey Island, but no clear indication of the path.

Louise goes over the top, following the random sign into the heath. Lucy and I retrace our steps to the gate to follow the guidebook.

A helpful gentleman, walking his dog, tells us that up ahead is very muddy. He suggests to take the road or stay high on Mynydd y Graig, which we do and the signs are clear again.

We cover the track to Rhiw quickly. A helpful National Trust volunteer at Plas y Rhiw tells us that it is impossible to access Hell's Mouth beach further down the road due to a landslide. He suggests we go past the National Trust car park and follow the lane.

He warns us that the beach boulders are very slippery and says to take care. He is right! Louise and I slide and slip our way across to the long sandy stretch, while Lucy ventures closer to the vulnerable crumbling cliffs, for a longer but safer crossing.

The Wales Coast Path takes you inland, but what a shame to miss out on Porth Neigwl/Hells Mouth.

Three tired women pick up the path again at the end of Hells Mouth and make our way to the Ship Inn to pick up the car. Catching sight of the super moon as we end a long day.

St Hywyn's Church, Aberdaron.

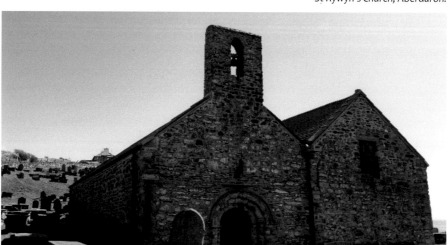

Aberdaron in winter.

Porthor (Whistling Sands) to Aberdaron

The Wales Coast Path is at its wildest, most remote and breathtaking, in both senses of the word. The views are spectacular, the gradients steep. A totally engrossing walk.

We start from the National Trust car park in Porthor. We walk between the toilet blocks, (thankfully open), onto the path. We are almost immediately out onto the clifftop path, leading to the heathland of Mynydd Anelog, down by an old wall, a little dog leg and down towards Porth Llan-llawen. The path wanders nicely along the coastal inlets.

Where there are gaps in the waymark signs, we just follow the most defined path up Mynydd Mawr. This is a steep one. At one stage it looks virtually perpendicular. It also has a false summit and we assume we have reached the top, but there is more climbing to follow, until we reach the coastguard station.

Once we reach the summit, there are splendid views across to Bardsey Island. It is quite thought provoking to think you are walking in the footsteps of pilgrims and of the souls of twenty thousand saints buried on the island.

The concrete road leading away from the coastguard station provides an easy descent, and the path takes us close to the edge around Braich y

Pwll, the very edge of Wales. We could do with a sign here to indicate that we are at 'Wales End'.

Following on over the common and then a rocky patch, we opt not to go in search of St Mary's Well, blessed by the Virgin Mary, so says the legend. It was blustery, and we were a bit reluctant to venture down to the shoreline.

The other place where we feel an additional sign would be useful is at Pen y Cil, where the instinct would be to turn inland, but the path continues onwards passing a cairn on the right.

Turning towards Aberdaron, we are glad to be sheltered from the wind. There is a steep walk down into Porth Meudwy, where the boats cross the sea to Bardsey in the summer.

It isn't long before we are walking down the steep set of steps to the beach at Aberdaron. We take one look at the steps leading up to the headland and decide to walk across the beach to the village, taking our chances with the stream dissecting the sands.

Porth Meudwy, with the boats to Bardsey Island.

We could be the only people on the Llŷn.

Porthor to Porth Ychain

A day of long shadows and bright winter sunshine. We have an early start, parking in the National Trust car park at Porthor (Whistling Sands). We set off at a brisk pace and it is all straightforward along the clifftops to Porth Iago.

We soon slow down as we make our way gingerly through the muddy tracks.

The joy of winter walking is that you hardly see a soul; the downside is you must put up with sometimes adverse conditions. Progress is slow.

We do moan when the path diverges inland, but it is not the case here as the path closely hugs the low shoreline. Along quite a long stretch of the Llŷn, the farmers have made good use of the land and there is little room to manoeuvre between the fence, path and sea. It makes walking in winter quite precarious at times.

Stories of the shipwrecked Stuart, an iron barque, keep us entertained as the path continues to Porth Widlin. The ship ran aground in 1901, with a bountiful cargo including whisky. Yet another whisky galore event along the Welsh coasts. The locals had the cargo away before the custom officials arrived from Caernarfon.

I am focusing so hard on the walk at the expense of enjoying the scenery. I stop and Whoomph! Fell! First reaction is to save the camera! Second is feeling so annoyed, having carefully negotiating through the mud slick to fall while standing in one place.

The Llŷn scenery does not disappoint. We are constantly in awe, reflecting on the remoteness, the proximity to the sea, and the solitude. The large sky is a fusion of pinks and blush, a delicate blue and the light is soft yet crystal clear.

There is a little harbour at Porth Colmon (small car park and access inland here) eventually leading down some steps and crossing the stream to cross Penllech beach. A few up and downs later we decide to leave the path at Porth Ychain as night was drawing in, it had taken us longer to walk than we anticipated due to the wintery conditions. We sensibly walk inland to Tudweilog, rather than be caught out on the headland in the dark.

Approaching the tip of the Llŷn and it is tough in parts.

Clear water to wipe off the worst of the mud.

Porth Ychgain to Morfa Nefyn

Have you ever heard *The Hippopotamus Song* by Flanders and Swann? The chorus goes like this: '*Mud, mud glorious mud. Nothing quite like it for cooling the blood. So follow me, follow down to the hollow. And there we can wallow in glorious mud*'.

It sums up the day! We are glad to have taken an 'early bath' the previous evening as the conditions under foot are appalling.

To fully appreciate the striking scenery, this section is probably best experienced between late spring and autumn, not in the height of winter following a period of rain. The path mainly consists of disparate tracks, little more than sheep tracks, the mud is congealed. We are grateful for the sturdy farmers' fences, which offer us leverage on several occasions. The path follows the low-lying cliffs, reaching some steps which we normally loathe. They come as a welcome relief from the relentless slog!

At Porth Ysgaden, we explore the remaining wall of a lime kiln. The tin sheds at Porth y Cychod are a source of curiosity, and near the popular beach at Porth Towyn.

Somewhere between Penrhyn Cwmistir and Aber Geirch, we come across a colony of spotted seals... such a delight, we stay and watch for

ages, so entertaining to watch the interplay.

In startling contrast to the early stages of this walk, is the appearance of Nefyn golf course in the distance. It is a bit of a scramble to access the course from the river below, but a welcome relief to skirt the edges of this beautifully manicured course.

Around Trwyn Porth Dinllaen and down to one of my favourite beaches in Wales, Porth Dinllaen. The well-known pub, featured on numerous tourism posters, is closed. The Ty Coch pub is on winter hours and is covered in scaffolding with men hard at work. To say we are disappointed would be an understatement.

One final walk across the bay to Morfa Nefyn and our bed for the night! During the day I fell twice in the mud and Lucy sank into the deep glutinous mud. It has been a dramatic, tiring day but, in a perverse way, enjoyable. Lucy sums up the day by quoting from Macbeth: 'I am in blood / Stepped in so far that should I wade no more, / Returning were as tedious as go o'er.'

(above) Porth Nefyn.
(opposite, bottom) The views from the hill above Nant Gwrtheyrn.

Morfa Nefyn to Nant Gwrtheyrn

We dither this morning, not quite sure whether we can hack a climb up the Eifl mountain. Our struggles with the mud the previous day having worn us out.

We settle for a walk to Nant Gwrtheyrn stopping for longer breaks than usual. For the first time ever, I use a walking pole, kindly supplied by Lucy, to take the stress off my bruised hip, sustained when I fell on an earlier walk. Despite my anti-walking pole comments of the past, I quickly become a convert.

A short stroll from our apartment, we access the steps leading to a clearly defined path across to the tiny headland at Penrhyn Nefyn and onwards to the small fishing harbour of Nefyn. In 1284 the English King Edward I held a jousting tournament in Nefyn when he defeated us Welsh.

St Mary's Church, currently a museum, would have been on the pilgrimage route to Bardsey Island.

The path heads inland, and we can see a sign indicating the path is closed. Generally, I wouldn't advise ignoring signs stating the path is closed, from experience it is dangerous. Additionally, by the time you turn around from an obstacle you have added miles to your day. This time though we can see that the work is complete, and we have no difficulty in walking onwards, until we reach the main road on the outskirts of the village of Pistyll. Turning left to cross the road we now follow the signs.

We pass a little church in a hollow, where Rupert Davis, the actor who played Maigret in the 1960s TV series, is buried.

We walk on above Porth Pistyll to Penrhyn Glas. We spy a sheep precariously clinging to the side of a rock, before we climb up to a ridge, then downwards through an ancient forest. It is so atmospheric. I half expect to see hobbits, goblins and wizards appear at any moment.

At Porth y Nant the remains of the granite quarry are clear to see, although the working men's cottages and allied buildings are now home to Nant Gwrtheyrn Welsh language and Heritage Centre.

King Vortigen was King of Britain in the fifth century, and it is said he hid here from his enemies. I get emotionally caught up in the tragic love story of Rhys and Meinir, a young couple who were due to get married. Tradition had it that the bride would go and hide on the morning of the wedding. The groom's friends would search for her and bring her to the altar, and the two would be married. They searched high and low but could not find the bride to be. Rhys spent months looking for Meinir and one night he rested under an oak tree when it was struck with lightening. It split open to reveal a skeleton wearing a wedding gown. Rhys died with shock on the spot.

Once at the Nant, we tackle the hard slog up the hill to the car park, passing the creaking, groaning pine trees. Another thoroughly satisfying day!

(above) Looking across the coast of north Wales.
(opposite) Legends of the lovers.

Nant Gwrtheyrn and Trefor

We got up early to tweet the sunrise, before leaving the car park at Porth Nant. We are conscious that we have a four hour journey home at the end of the day.

There isn't a soul around and there is a biting wind. Looking down, we can see Nant Gwrtheyrn in the valley below, and the steep hill we dragged our sorry selves up the previous day...

We climb steadily towards Bwlch yr Eifl, before extending our walk up towards the microwave station to take in the views across North Wales.

Lucy compares me to her dad as I am now using her walking pole to point out various landmarks. It sounds as if the O'Donnell children are lucky not to have their eyes poked out through Mr O'D's enthusiastic use of his stick.

On that highest point on the Wales Coast Path, we part company. I head up hill to the Eifl (564 mts) and Lucy downhill towards Trefor. Reaching the top, the low visibility obliterate any views. It is very Game of Thrones-ish, with the swirling low clouds. Where is Jon Snow? I abandon the trek to the Iron Age settlement of Tre'r Ceiri to another day.

Heading downhill is harder going. The loose stones give way under foot.

Trefor Harbour.

The sun comes out, but too late to turn back for another attempt at Tre'r Ceiri.

As I pass Bwlch yr Eifl, a group of walkers are making their way uphill in a long line.

The front runners make a swift pace, while the stragglers at the back seem to be having more fun talking, laughing and walking. We had a chatty break; they are from Prestatyn and interested in our slow Wales Coast Path ramble.

I leave the moor and pass a ruined miners' cottage, and from then on it is an easy walk down the path, followed by a lane and a couple of fields. At the road I am confused by the next sign. It seems to say that I should be heading back up the mountain towards the brooding Eifl Granite Quarries, but the path takes me on a dog leg to get to the white-washed West End cottages, reaching a very pleasant stretch along the cliffs to the pretty harbour at Trefor.

Catching up with Lucy, we are both glad that we decided to walk down into Trefor as opposed to walking up hill from the harbour, easier on the knees!

Along the A499 – seemed endless, but the beauty of Llŷn is in sight.

Dinas Dinlle to Trefor

We struggle to find many positives in this walk. We remind ourselves of the difficulties in creating a coast path, but even this doesn't make us feel charitable. We should have spent more time enjoying the views across to Anglesey and the Llŷn, and exploring the precariously placed hill fort at Dinas Dinlle, as there is nothing much to please the eye for the next few miles.

We head for the A499. Most of the route straddles the busy main road.

We follow an easy walk with a paved path, which also doubles as a cycle route. We occasionally take the old road through villages and then return to the A499.

We needed to be alert! Having passed the junction for Penygroes, at the next junction there is a left, and right turn in quick succession.

The highlight of the route is St Bueno's Church at Clynnog Fawr. A great example of a Tudor Church, almost cathedral in size. Sir Clough Ellis Williams, who masterminded Portmeirion, said that this church inspired him to be an architect. It is well worth a visit.

(above) St Bueno's church.
(below) Old mile marker.

A little further along is St Bueno's Well, one of the healing wells in Wales. This would have been close to the Pilgrim route to Bardsey Island.

We are reminded that we are following in the steps of pilgrims travelling to Bardsey. The church and well would have had massive religious significance on this route.

We are very relieved to turn off the main road towards Trefor and the final mile of the walk.

Caernarfon Castle approaching from Y Foryd.

Dinas Dinlle to Caernarfon

This walk is at low levels, no major inclines to challenge us. As mentioned frequently we are not fans of road walking, and much of this stretch is along tarmac, but it is comfortable, easy walking after a few challenging days.

Leaving Dinas Dinlle we follow the paved path along the shoreline and pass the Caernarfon Airworld Aviation Museum. We approach the caravan park, and carry straight on into a grassy lane, then left to take us all the way around to a footbridge over Afon Carrog, eventually heading by road inland to Saron.

We have a water stop on the bridge over Afon Gwyrfai.

Our favourite part of this walk is alongside Foryd bay, another great spot for bird watchers. A brisk wind is blowing – today is not a day for spotting the difference between a widgeon or a wild fowl. Rain is in the air, but I stop for a chat with a local farmer, he tells me authoritatively we will make it to Caernarfon before the rain.

Nothing can prepare you for the sight of Caernarfon's walls and castle built by Edward I to subdue the Welsh. The Iron Ring of Castles is an over-the-top statement of intent by a king determined to dominate this western corner of what he considered to be his kingdom. The castle itself is impressive, whatever one thinks of its history. The four castles of Harlech, Beaumaris, Conway and Caernarfon have been designated UNESCO world heritage status. Approaching from the Foryd, it is a view that is unfamiliar to us. Since Edward I designated his son as Prince of Wales, the title has been inherited by heirs to the throne of England. Caernarfon was the scene of Prince Charles's investiture as the Prince of Wales.

We don't head for the mighty castle, but the Bar Bach, the smallest bar in Wales for a shot of Penderyn Whisky to warm us up.

Sure enough, snug in the bar, the winds roar and the sky opens. Nothing for it but to have dinner at the Black Boy.

This short hike completes the Llŷn Peninsula, but the drama doesn't stop there.

It has snowed overnight and Caernarfon is a winter wonderland. Lucy gets up at 5.00am to beat the weather for her drive home, as more of the white stuff is promised. I rest up for another couple of hours as I am heading across North Wales to join friends for a short break.

Setting off after breakfast, I end up with a puncture outside Caernarfon. I evaluated my options, waiting for the RAC in a cold lay-by or calling a local garage. I am familiar with the Celtic Royal Hotel and decide to seek help there, risking the short drive with a flat tire in the snow. They soon sort me out, offering coffee and ringing a local garage, telling me to make myself comfortable as they will call me when the recovery chaps arrives. Their combined help means I am on the road at lunchtime. Too early to check into our self-catering, so I wallow in the warmth of the cinema in Llandudno Junction, enjoying my popcorn and *Paddington 2*.

Y Foryd.

Looking across at Felinheli.

North Wales – Caernarfon to Chester – 78 miles – 126kms
Bwrw hen wragedd a ffyn – Raining old wives and walking sticks – Raining cats and dogs.

Y Felinheli and Caernarfon

The Felinheli or Port Dinorwic, as it is often referred to in English, sits on the mainland of Wales beside the Menai Straits. It is our home for the next few days as we tread the Wales Coast Path once again.

A taxi driver tells us that Felinheli means salt mill. *Felin* means mill and *helo* means salt water or brine. Then again, the name could mean the mill on the Heulyn, which is the river that runs through the village.

The small modern marina is a far cry from the days when slate from the nearby Dinorwic quarry used to be transferred by rail to the quay then loaded and shipped across the world.

We arrive late afternoon, so a short four mile walk to Caernarfon to limber up for the next few days, followed by dinner, seems a good idea.

It isn't an auspicious start as we turn right instead of left! Surprise, surprise a VW Beetle comes up the road, my old friend Gwenda at the wheel.

I have not seen her in years, last heard of in Ireland. We have a short gossip and promise to catch up later. This is what Wales is like, you invariably run into someone you know.

On the right track, we walk along the busy A487, before we join the cycle path for the four mile stretch into Caernarfon.

The Welsh flag is flying high over Caernarfon Castle as we make our way to our favourite pub, The Black Boy. On the wall of the pub, the sign tells us that this used to be the red-light district. The Welsh name for the street is *Stryd Pedwar a Chwech* which literally means Four and Six Street. In old shillings and pence, a sailor could get a room, a woman and a bottle of gin for this price...

NOT THE CASE TODAY!

Lucy is highly amused as I could have devoured the whole menu, and quote the items out loud, a hungry woman's mantra, before eventually settling for good old fish and chips.

Over dinner we talk about the so-called Iron Ring of Castles, and the fortification of the North Wales coast by Edward I. Strategically they couldn't have been built in a better place with a supply route from the sea. He had sent his forces into battle twice against Llywelyn the Last and won. He was not taking any risks with any further rebellions, and while happy to 'refresh' existing castles in the rest of Wales, he knew that the biggest threat was from those loyal to the Princes of Gwynedd and their family.

His building programme, costing in the region of £35 million in today's money, almost bankrupted the state. He populated the bastions with English settlers and the Welsh were only allowed in during the day, but not to trade, which would have meant that times were hard indeed for the locals.

I wonder what he would have made of the thousands of tourists who pass through the castle gates every day, where the flag of Wales flies high on the wind.

After dinner we order a taxi to take us back to Felinheli. The driver is pondering why it is so busy for a Thursday. He is worried he won't be able get to his stir-fry takeaway supper until around 10pm, and by then he would probably settle for a corn beef sandwich! We love the Cofis (the people of Caernarfon)

A Warm Welcome

In the town's heyday as a port, Northgate Street was the heart of the red-light district. Its Welsh name is Stryd Pedwar a Chwech literally translates to Four and Six Street, which in old Shillings and pence is what a sailor had to pay for a room, a bottle of gin and a woman for the night.
The street contains the Black Boy Inn which it is claimed dates back to 1522. One theory regarding its name is that it's after a black buoy that used to be found in the

View of Bangor Pier.

Abergwyngregyn to Felinheli

The morning mist shrouds the nature reserve below Abergwyngregyn and our breath billows in the air. Setting off briskly, it is just as well we don't know that our twelve mile walk will stretch to fifteen as the day goes on.

We set a quick a pace along Traeth Lamar, quickly reaching the Spinnies nature reserve. The nature reserves from Llanfairfechan to the Spinnies are well worth another visit!

We see Penrhyn Castle in the distance, and for much of the next hour we skirt the estate. It would have been so much nicer if we could have cut through the property, rather than detour through to Talybont and Bryn.

Somewhere in crossing the main road from Bryn we lose sight of the signs and have to track back a couple of times, before reaching Porth Penrhyn. Slate from Penrhyn Slate Quarry used to be transported, first by railway from the quarry to the port, and then onwards.

We continue up the junction to the A5 and reach the Garth in Bangor, with its impressive pier. At one thousand five hundred feet it is some eight hundred and fifty feet shorter than LLandudno Pier, known to be the longest pier in Wales. An optical illusion makes you think that the pier reaches out as far as Anglesey. This is not the case.

The path does not go into Bangor, but descends to the shoreline. It then follows along towards Nant Borth, once a limestone quarry now a nature reserve, through the woodland, then up passing a ruin and then a soccer training ground.

Back out on the A5 we head for Menai Suspension Bridge, and the road to Anglesey. We continue towards the Britannia Bridge, opened in 1850 and designed by Robert Stephenson as a rail bridge. It is only in the 1970s that it is adapted to take both road and rail traffic.

Glad to leave the A487, we seek a more attractive route through the Faenol Estate. We follow the signs through the estate and discover that if we head right up the field, as directed, there is no obvious route. We ask some local walkers and they direct us back down the field to follow a well-cut path by the Straits. They say it will take us to Felinheli. What they don't say is that we will be confronted by a five-bar gate, topped with another five-bar metal structure. We retrace our steps, only to confront another sign saying KEEP OUT.

Fortunately, the owner arrives, and kindly points us in the right direction, and after a bit of maneuvering we arrive at our final stop. A robin pops his head out, as if to say, 'Well done, ladies.' Louise, who is walking with us, is probably wondering how we got this far? The back tracking and wrong turns probably mean that we have walked well beyond the eight hundred and seventy miles of the Wales Coast Path.

While we outline our journey here in geographic order, we don't walk the path in a linear fashion. As mentioned earlier we take a more flexible approach, allowing us to join up with friends, eat at a choice of restaurants, seek out local happenings; the whole essence of slow walking is to enjoy!

We had started our North Wales leg earlier in the year in Chester, moved down to South Wales where we were able to sneak walking days here and there, and then back to North Wales for several short breaks, as and when we could. We wanted to complete our walk on the Isle of Anglesey. So this is actually the final stretch of the Welsh mainland.

Long before this stage, while walking Gower, the Wales Coast Path had developed a personality of its own! We frequently referred to the path as 'she' – as in 'She's not happy' or having cursed the path and the vagaries of the signage and the occasional counter-intuitive route, we have become convinced that the path had a life and will of its own. If we criticise her in any way, she becomes contrary and puts more obstacles in our way. Or so it seemed to us at the time.

Lucy comments, 'The Path really doesn't want to let go of us' and in truth it is like waving farewell to a very good friend.

We stay at a super house on the Felinheli, and in the evening, we have dinner at the local pub, the Garddfon Inn. Desperate Dan would have been delighted with the size and quality of my Welsh beef steak.

(opposite) Menai Suspension Bridge.

(above) Sandstorm at Conwy Morfa.
(opposite, top) Hopping around near Llanfairfechan.
(opposite, bottom) A welcome at Abergwyngregyn.

Conwy Marina to Abergwyngregyn

It is officially British Summer Time; the days are longer, and the sun is shining. The Beast from the East is forecasted for a few days' time. Slow walking gives way to speedy, as we need to cover a few miles along the north Wales coast.

We selected the blue route (the red route through Sychnant Pass is a walk for another day!)

We walk along the beach from Conwy Morfa. We could have walked along the beach as far as Penmaenmawr, but we are wary of the tides and the soft sand.

Such is our relationship with the Wales Coast Path, we must follow the signs, considering ourselves disloyal if we deviate. We leave the beach and rejoin the path at Penmaenbach and work our way through a network of bridges and cycle paths, heading high over the A55. A marvel of engineering and effort.

We stop for coffee at the café in Penmaenmawr. The vivid street art helps balance the brutalist architecture.

The pretty village of Llanfairfechan is soon reached. The Victorian school with the separate entrance for boys and girls, the independent shops, and the chapels add a certain charm. We then head under the bridge to the promenade. We watch a chap feed the swans by the pond, before following the track to Morfa Madryn and a network of nature reserves.

We reach the car park and are greeted by a smiling George Clooney. On a poster advert drinking a brand of coffee, a welcome sight, nonetheless.

Our home is well-placed on Conwy Marina, a modern house. It is a bit like living in a goldfish bowl. Behind the tinted windows, we are able to watch the curious visitors who try to peer in through the glass.

(above) Conwy Castle.
(opposite, bottom) Alice in Wonderland at Llandudno.

Conwy Marina to Llandudno

Balmy breeze and warm sunshine. How changeable can our weather be? We have given ourselves an easy day walking, a short stroll in the sunshine. The Wales Coast Path passes by our home for the holiday in Conwy marina, making it so easy. We stroll along Conwy Quays passing Bodlondeb nature reserve, stopping for photographs in front of the 'smallest house in Great Britain'. We wonder whether it has ever been any colour but red?

Meanly, we chuckle as a seagull attacks a woman trying to eat her fish and chips.

The stroll takes us past the lobster pots on the Quay, up a few steps to the walkway alongside the road. We then look across at the original Telford Bridge built in 1826.

It is only a little distance along the walkway that you appreciate the full scale of Conwy Castle, another one of Edward I's Iron Ring of Castles. Richly deserving of its UNESCO world heritage site status, it still elicits an emotional response from me. I suspect it has something to do with difficulties at school trying to remember the achievements of eleven King Edwards, eight King Henrys, three King Charles, three King Richard and two King James, but hang on there, were six of those in Scotland? The only one I can remember with some depth is Edward I – Longshanks and his position in Welsh history. Oh, Henry Tudor, Henry VII because of his birth at Pembroke Castle, and Elizabeth I – she was one of my heroines.

Looking up at the impressive build I want to sing the song by Dafydd Iawn, a famous Welsh folk singer.

'*Er gwaetha pawb a phopeth, ry'n ni yma o hyd.*' Roughly translated it means, 'Despite everyone and everything, we are still here.'

The promenade and cycle track give great views across the estuary of the walled town of Conwy and the mountains beyond.

At a leisurely pace, enjoying the scenic backdrop to Deganwy, we drop onto the West Shore in Llandudno.

The White Rabbit memorial is a reminder that Alice Liddell's holiday home was here, and she was the inspiration behind Lewis Carroll's *Alice in Wonderland*. The book has been enjoyed by several generations of children.

Our leisurely day is followed by an equally leisurely evening starting at the Albion pub, dating from the 1920s, owned by local small brewers and serving a variety of local beers. *The Observer* newspaper said it was the best pub in the world. We love the Smoking Room sign on the door, a reminder of bygone times.

We follow this with a short stroll to the Erskine Arms, a Georgian coaching inn. We dine on locally sourced cockles and mussels, fish and pork.

Both places have the friendliest staff, and we're told that on a rainy, cold night there are welcoming open fires. Sometimes you must let go of the longer-term goal and pause to enjoy the now!

(above) The RNLI at Llandudno.
(opposite, bottom) The Kashmiri goats of Llandudno.

Colwyn Bay to Llandudno

Work is underway to dismantle the Victorian pier on the curved golden sands of the bay between Porth Eirias to Llandrillo yn Rhos/Rhos on Sea.

Embedded into the walkway are some historic facts. One states that Prince Madog sailed from here and discovered America three hundred years before Columbus.

At Rhos on Sea, I stop to visit the tiny church of St Trillo, seating only six people. It must be the smallest church in Wales, if not Britain. Flowers are on the alter. A place for quiet contemplation.

Lucy is powering ahead towards Penrhyn Bay. I rush to catch up as I am keen to go out to the headland to look for seals. Half a dozen can be seen huddled and well-camouflaged on the rocks below.

Turning back, we take the short but steep slope up the Little Orme and head through the quarries, before quickly coming down Craigside, to the roadside and an easy walk into Llandudno.

We pause in the bitter wind to watch the brave RNLI lifeboat crew man their boat, before wandering on and veering off the path into the Mostyn Gallery for coffee, cake and a look around their exhibition.

Llandudno has done much to preserve its Victorian charm, and we return to the Promenade making our way to the pier, skirting around to Marine Drive, which takes us up the Great Orme.

The road is closed to traffic, but we are soon joined by the seven hundred or so participants in the Nick Beer 10k road race.

While we are highly entertained by this procession, the Kashmiri goats that roam the headland do not take a blind bit of notice of the spectacle, as they continue to graze on the uplands.

Passing the road access to the lighthouse, now a B&B, we stop for a breather at the aptly named Rest and Be Thankful café (and we were). We pour tea from one of those stainless-steel tea pots, the ones that seem to have a design fault as the tea drips past the lid!

We share a laugh with fellow customers as we watch the walkers being swirled around by the wind, while knowing we will soon be engaged in a similar pantomime.

Rounding the headland, there are stunning views across to east Anglesey and the Carneddau mountains. On the way down we overlook an old military site.

Reaching the Gatehouse to the Gogarth we hurry along West Shore beach frozen to the core, grateful to reach the car.

A varied walk, enjoyable even in the high winds, but probably preferable in warmer weather!

(above) Kinmel Bay beach.
(opposite, left) St Trillo's Chapel, Rhos on Sea.

Kinmel Bay and Colwyn Bay

It might be the weather, or it could be been down to our tired, weary selves, but we are not inspired by this stretch of the Wales Coast Path. We enjoy a very pleasant evening in Prestatyn in our rental bungalow, with friendly host/owners, plenty of information about local restaurants, and things to do.

We are glad of the torrential early morning rain, which sees us starting our walk later than usual.

Out to sea, standing like sentries on the horizon, are hundreds of wind turbines. Turning to look inland, we are faced with row upon row of caravans, coupled with grey skies. This is not a walk to lighten our spirits. We remind ourselves that it isn't all about the view. Thousands enjoy great times in these caravans every year, and while on a grey winter's day it is not easy on the eye, the summer sees the beaches and amusement arcades busy with families out for a good time.

The path runs along cycle track five, a bonus as we cover the miles quickly. A large breakfast at the beach café at Pensarn in Abergele, served by cheerful, polite young staff puts some pep back in our step.

Gwrych Castle comes into view, looking across the A55 towards the limestone cliffs. It reminds Lucy of Disneyland and I think of Grimm's fairy tales.

A family on bikes approach us, followed by several others. The older kids must have had big bikes for Christmas, as they are still a bit wobbly. We smile and our mood lifts marginally. Several other cyclists whizz by. It makes me feel positive, the cycle route is an asset and well-used.

The traffic on the North Wales expressway is also a bit of an irritant, but at Llandulais the cycle track climbs a little before passing by the Raynes jetty that handles the limestone from the quarry across the road.

Rain brings our walk to an end at Porth Eirias where we pop into Welsh chef Bryn Williams' restaurant, but we are a bit late to be served. It has been that sort of day!

(below) Historic facts along Colwyn Bay beach.
(underneath) Iron statues on Colwyn Bay promenade.

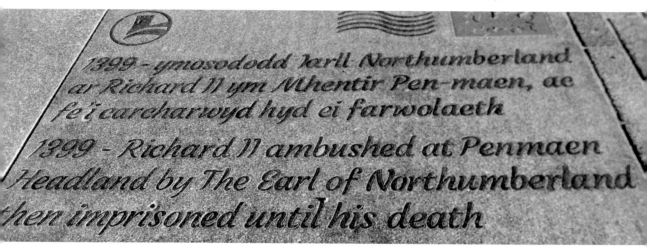

Talacre Lighthouse.

Ffynnongroyw to Kinmel Bay

Snow is forecast, but we are wrapped up warm and ready to go! The winding gear from the Number two shaft of the Point of Ayr colliery has been restored and sits proudly near FFynongroyw by the busy A548. Crossing the road, we are soon out on the exposed wasteland of the Point of Ayr Colliery, the area was known as Y Parlwr Du – the Black Parlour, not a cosy Victorian parlour then or now.

A hailstorm slaps us in the face. There is a bitterly cold wind. A large gasworks looms, as we hurry down towards Talacre from the Point of Ayr, the most northerly point on mainland North Wales. I have never felt so cold or miserable, and from Lucy's expression she isn't enjoying it much either.

At the car park, the dog walkers are out in force, reminding us of a certain Peter Kaye car comedy sketch. You must find humour even on the coldest of days. We head up to the viewpoint but decide to keep off the beach. This is the first or last beach in Wales, depending on your direction of travel.

We follow the low tide route through the dunes, which offer a little protection against the wind. Slightly distorted by the mizzle is Talacre lighthouse, grade II listed and haunted. Tales of footsteps in the sand, and a man spotted in old fashion clothing, thought to be Raymond, a long dead

The Point of Ayr on a snowy day.

lighthouse keeper. I am happy to believe anything on a ghostly day like today. The lighthouse looks in need of a good paint job.

We head for the Gronant dunes at Prestatyn Haven Sands Holiday Park. The dunes have a noted inhabitant, the natterjack toad. No self-respecting toad is to be seen out on such a cold day.

Following a walkway, we find ourselves on Barkby Beach, passing some marsh land, then heading back as quickly as we can to the shelter of the dunes. The sky by now is bright blue, but the sharp hail showers, and a biting wind has us hurrying to the Beaches Hotel for a warming lunch of Welsh cawl.

From here, it is a straightforward promenade, following a concrete walkway along Ffrith Beach, passing the jolly holiday towns of Prestatyn and Rhyl. At the very modern Pavilion building in Rhyl, we are delighted to step inside and warm up.

The walkway continues across the footbridge to Kinmel Bay ending a very cold winter's walk.

The King and his dog, Flint Castle.

Flint to Ffynnongroyw

We have an adverse weather forecast for the day ahead. We miss the rain completely just by getting up at the crack of dawn. The changeable conditions have us now packing for four seasons in one day.

We start at Flint castle, the first of Edward I strongholds in Wales. Construction began in 1277 around the same time as the beginning of the first Welsh war in 1277 against LLywelyn the Last, and mainly completed by 1284.

I am enjoying the location, the history and the views across the estuary towards England.

We find this an easy walk, as it must have been for the king's men marching to Flint from the garrison at Chester.

It is hard to believe that the silted Flint Dock used to be a busy harbour, built to carry lead from the mines in Halkyn mountain. Hardly anyone or anything moved as we walked past. The information boards are extremely helpful in outlining the history of the area. In fact, I would go as far as to say that it is the best interpretation we have seen to date.

In 1778 a ship carrying grain was taken over by local miners, as there was

(above) The steel dragon looking out on the Dee.
(opposite, right) Public art along the river Dee.

a shortage of food, mainly bread. Given the severe hardship it seemed to be the only thing they could do. I suspect their punishment was harsh.

The beacons along this stretch are nicely designed; the most impressive is the dragon beacon at Bagillt, built to celebrate the Wales Coast Path.

Not a day to linger, we set a brisk pace passing Bettisfield Colliery now a scrap yard. The inspector of mines list for 1896 records that five hundred and thirty-eight men worked here.

Onto Greenfield Dock. This used to be a lively link for pilgrims from Liverpool, Wirral and surrounding areas who used to take the waters at nearby St Winifred's Well, Holywell.

At Llanerch y Mor we come across the Duke of Lancaster – the ship not the person. Docked here as a Fun ship in the 1970s, it had previously been used as a ferry from Belfast to Haysham. It is rusting badly now and looks rather sad.

Beyond the ship, we spot hundreds, if not thousands, of oystercatchers nesting. I may have mentioned numerous times the delight of birdwatching while winter walking.

We take the easy option along the cycle track, past the busy Mostyn Dock. In hindsight we should have taken the higher route through the woods, as this turns out to be a busy road, with fast moving traffic. We breathe a sigh of relief when we reach the village of Ffynongroyw (Clear Well). The well itself can be accessed via the aptly called Well Lane.

The village happens to be the birthplace of renowned Welsh harpist Osian Ellis.

We end our day fittingly, at the commemoration to the Point of Ayr Colliery, the last deep pit to close in North Wales, as this walk is a poignant reminder of Flint's rich industrial past.

(above) Queensferry or Jubilee Bridge.
(opposite) Welcome to Wales on a windy day.

Chester to Flint

One of our earlier forays onto the Wales Coast Path ties into a girlie weekend in Chester. We are still figuring out how to best tackle this new adventure. By the time we return to South Wales we have learned quite a few lessons. The do's and don'ts of walking.

We start the walk around 1pm. I am staying with friends in North Wales, and I drive across to Chester to pick up Lucy and our friend Kim from the train station. We deposit our stuff at a lovely AirBnb property before we set off, optimistically hoping to get some walking done before the promised rain forecast for 5pm.

We make our way out of Chester via the Town Hall. The town clock is said to have only three faces, as the citizens of Chester didn't feel the need to have one facing Wales, as they couldn't be bothered to spare the Welsh the time of day. There was a time when the Welsh were forbidden to enter Chester before sunrise or to stay out after nightfall, but no such curfew applies today. Hordes of shoppers from North Wales regularly descend on Chester, and we find the people of Chester to be helpful, charming and welcoming.

We carry on via Northgate, past Pemberton Tower and the Water Tower. It is easy to see that Chester is one of the best-preserved walled cities in Britain.

The Wales Coast Path ostensibly starts just outside Chester, while the city of course is in England. The daffodils smile in the wind as we reach the Welcome to Wales sign. We then follow a straightforward, long straight stretch on the cycle path, beside the river Dee.

The rain comes early. An hour into the walk we are soaked to the skin. We give up at the Jubilee Bridge or Blue Bridge at Queensferry and trudge to the nearest bus stop. After a lengthy wait for a bus that never comes, we call a taxi to get us back to our townhouse. We are looking more like the female cast of *Last of the Summer Wine* than the cosmopolitan women we perceive ourselves to be.

Our walking gear never quite dries out overnight. It isn't pleasant getting up next morning and into damp, cold hiking gear. Out on the path we can now see the four towers of Connah's Quay power station. The guidebook specifies the towers as the key landmark for the walk, with our chances of seeing them through the gloom and the rain being nil.

So, back to the Jubilee Bridge, a bascule bridge, sparkling blue in the sunshine. This stretch of Wales Coast Path is mainly dominated by industry, so from bridge to bridge we go, Jubilee, then Hawarden Railway Bridge, built by the Manchester, Sheffield and Lincolnshire Railways, originally as a swing bridge, but now welded solid! Didn't we say that bridges were a particular favourite.

The warmest temperature in Wales was recorded as 35.2 centigrade here in August 1990. We could have done with a bit more warmth on a chilly February day!

Our walk over, we morph into a trio of cosmopolitan city ladies, and in the late afternoon 'shop 'til we drop'. We run into our friend Esther, who joins us for a drink at the Grosvenor Hotel, before heading off for a hairdresser appointment.

It is our final morning in this fine city and we head for the other bridge on the skyline, the Flintshire Bridge, the largest asymmetrical bridge in Britain, opened in 1998, and built at a cost of £55 million. A testament to the importance of the industrial Deeside and its impact on the Welsh economy. The path continues past the Wepre riverside SSSI, and the site of the Old Quay Pub.

Much of the final leg of the walk is along the road, not terribly interesting, until we finally return to the marshes and come upon Flint Castle. The design of this castle is quite different from the rest of Edward I's domineering castle portfolio. In fact it is the only one of its kind in Britain and described as a 'classic, carret, savoyard'. The castle was burnt down by the custodian in 1294 to avoid it falling into the hands of Madog ap Llywelyn and his Welsh followers. Lucy bursts into an extract from Shakespeare's *Henry IV* as we approach the castle. It was here Henry Bolingbroke, son of John of Gaunt, captured Richard II in 1399.

'Fake news' is not a new phenomenon. Richard's reputation has been given a bad press over time. If you were king from the age of ten years you would also make a few mistakes along the way. He wasn't all bad, but seems to have gone off the rails between 1397 and 1399, his tyrannical years. There is a legend associated with Richard's dog, which apparently was loyal to Richard and never strayed from his side. When Henry came to Flint, the dog left Richard's side and lay down at Henry's feet.

I think I might have taken a bit of liberty with the story, but you get the gist.

The Bull Hotel, Beaumaris.

Isle of Anglesey 133.50 miles – 215km
Môn Mam Cymru – Anglesey the Mother of Wales
Dyfal Donc a Dyr Y Garreg – Constant Tapping Breaks the Stone.

Beaumaris to Menai Bridge

We wanted to complete the Wales Coast Path on the Island of Anglesey. I'd always been fascinated by its mystical past. This fertile island grew enough wheat to feed the people of Wales. The Romans must have realised that cutting off the food route would bring the rest of Wales to its knees. While securing Anglesey would also give them access to the sea route to Ireland. This mighty empire also felt threatened by those of the old faith, the Druids. Bloody battles ensued, first in 60/61AD, but Boudica or Buddug as she was known in Wales, was kicking off near Londinium. The Romans retreated to deal with that threat. Agricola steps in to finish things off in 77AD, putting an end to the nature worshiping Celtic religion, by massacring the Druids.

We find ourselves in the village of Menai Bridge on a Sunday with only 133.50 miles to go around the Isle of Anglesey before completing the Wales Coast Path. We decide to build up an appetite for lunch by taking a stroll from Beaumaris to Menai Bridge, followed by a Sunday lunch. This would set us up nicely for a couple of strenuous days walking.

Away from the promenade, there is a bit of a hill start to the walk, passing Baron Hill Golf Course.

Much of this walk is along a minor road, but there is a very boggy, muddy patch to get through before we reach an easy stretch through the village of Llandegfan, where Aled Jones used to live as a child. Neither of us were sopranos so the locals were spared a rendition of *Walking in the Air*.

We pass Porth y Wrach (Witches Port) and wonder what the story is behind the name. It is busy with enthusiastic men launching their boats. Over lunch we are told that it isn't *gwrach* as in witch, but derived from the wrasse fish. The area is now known as Menai Bridge Slipway. Such a boring explanation as my fertile imagination had given way to spells, drownings and other colourful tales.

Eventually reaching and crossing the Menai Suspension Bridge, a Thomas Telford design opened in 1826. We head for the Antelope pub in Bangor overlooking the Menai Straits for a drink. The pub has guitar lessons on a Sunday, and several locals of differing ability and age groups are in session.

We spend a happy hour listening to the jamming session, and reluctantly take our leave of the musicians and head for Beaumaris.

Beaumaris Castle, the last of Edward I castle fortification is centre stage, but we are making for the Bull Hotel for Sunday lunch. We are ravenous after the morning exertions.

Britannia Bridge.

A view over the Menai.

Over lunch the conversation drifts from one topic to another. Why have we got a French sounding name for a town built on marshland, on an island off the coast of North Wales? It was not always called Beaumaris, as a Viking hamlet it had gone by the name of Porth y Wygyr.

In 1295 work started on the castle and township. The Norman French builders, working under the guidance of the chief architect James St George started to call it Beaux Marais, for fair or beautiful marsh and the name has stood the test of time.

Beaumaris Castle is supposed to be the most perfect concentric castle, even though it was never finished. Probably because Edward I in 1296 had to turn his attention to the invasion of Scotland to take on William Wallace, better known as Braveheart, in battle.

The castle is a rather squat building in comparison to the other castles in the Iron Ring. The walls never reached the height required, as money was running scarce and by 1330 the work was discontinued.

We concluded over lunch that Edward I had used a sledgehammer to crack a nut. The size and strength of the build was ridiculously over the top and unnecessary for the intended task. Llywelyn the Last had been killed in battle near Cilmeri in 1282. Yet Edward I persisted in continuing to build these mighty fortresses, almost bankrupting his kingdom, and leaving his son and heir with massive monetary issues.

The castles were hardly used for real military purpose, or permanently lived in by royalty. Their use was more for storage and accommodation, and they were left virtually redundant within a generation.

Leaving the history aside, the castle built on a beautiful marsh is still pleasing on the eye. This is probably why so many artists visited the site during the romantic period. J W Turner famously painted the castle in 1835.

Menai Bridge with St Tysilio's church.

Dwyran and Menai Bridge

It is a beautiful spring day as we access the path from the main road at Dwyran, following the yellow and green sign near a house called Llwyn Helyg.

We are a bit nervous. The last time we followed a yellow and green sign rather than the Wales Coast Path signs, we ended up in the bogs of mid-Wales – to this day known as Bog-Gate!

We refer to our guidebook instructions constantly until we see the first of the Wales Coast Path signs. We discover that the Anglesey Coast Path is well signposted, which gives us confidence to abandon the guidebook and follow the signs.

Following field, farm tracks and roads, we pass the Anglesey Riding Centre, where the horses are munching contentedly on their hay. We are surprised at the clear view directly across to Caernarfon Castle.

Eventually we join the road just past the former Mermaid Inn. Beyond this is the Tan y Foel ferry that ran across the Straits to Caernarfon taking passengers to market and workers across the Straits. It closed in 1952.

Near this spot the Romans invaded Anglesey in 77AD and massacred the Druids.

The road passes the entrance to Anglesey Sea Zoo and Anglesey Sea Salt. It is too early into the walk to stop, a decision we later regret, as there are very few refreshment opportunities along the way.

As we approach Llandinan House we chance upon two local ladies. They inform us that the tide is out, so we can walk along the shoreline on the low tide route.

We run into these ladies again when we detour off the main route to the hamlet of Moel y Don. They are interested in our long-distance walk. One of them is looking for a retirement challenge. They loved our slow walking concept and figure they would start off by walking more of Anglesey, tying it in with the kind of indulgences we have enjoyed: local food, events, shopping and a bit of culture. We have converts!

We stop for a while at Moel y Don, taking in the views across to Felinheli. I spend a bit of time photographing a duck sitting on her nest, under the watchful eye of the duck's partner.

Centuries after the Romans, the bloody battle of Moel y Don took place here in 1282. Known as the Battle of the Bridge of Boats, two thousand infantrymen and two hundred cavalry were sent by Edward I to control Anglesey, and cut off food supplies. It was one of the last Welsh victories, as Edward's men preferred to face the sea than Llewellyn the Last's army and many drowned or were killed with arrows. Never-ending trauma for the islanders! Today it is so peaceful; it is hard to believe that so much blood has been shed on this spot.

We return to the path, passing St Edwen's Church. St Edwen established a church on this spot in the seventh century. She was an Anglo Saxon princess, daughter of Edwin, King of Northumbria. Heading across the crossroad on the A4080 towards Bryn Celli Ddu (Mound of the Dark Grove), a reconstructed burial chamber dating from the Neolithic age. Only a slight departure from the path, but truly an essential divergence, a site of historic significance. Early morning summer solstice will see the sunlight shine down the passageway into the inner tomb.

Some calves are drinking from the stream. We pause by a wooden footbridge as there are a plethora of signs. Guidebook in hand we head up through the next two fields, but are a bit flummoxed by an electric fence barring our way. Cautiously we touch the fence with one gloved finger to see if it is switched on. It might not have been the wisest of moves, but as it didn't trigger a sharp shock, we were able to find a suitable spot to slide under the wire and find the farm track referred to in our book.

We have never liked fields much, and the ones on some of those large estates on Anglesey can be huge. We are frequently seen walking around the circumference, Lucy in one direction, me another, looking for the style or gateway adding miles to our day.

The next stage follows much of the main road, but behind a small hedgerow, with duckboards in part. At low tide we take the permissive path down to the shoreline. This is a lovely stretch passing the statue of Lord Nelson, in the shadow of Britannia Bridge, then through the churchyard of St Mary's Church, which gave Llanfairpwllgwyngyllgogerychwyrndrobwlll-lantysiliogogogoch its name.

Turning right in front of the Carreg Bran Hotel, some tree cutting is taking place in the wood. The path circles back to the road to Menai Bridge and you might think you are at the end of the journey, but it tracks down to the left again passing Church Island.

It has been a long day and Lucy decides to head into Menai Bridge while I go and investigate St Tysilio's Church and churchyard dating from the fifteenth century.

Failing to find the grave of Cynan, one of Wales's most prominent poets, I hurry to message Lucy to find out whether she was at the Liverpool Arms or Dylan's. I find her (with a glass of wine and her boots off) in Dylan's looking out across the straits; she had cornered a seat with a view.

We haven't had much time to explore the shops but make up for it by visiting a lighting shop run by Anglesey Paper Company. They sell the most gorgeous paper goods and lighting.

(below) Statue of Lord Nelson in the shadow of Britannia Bridge.
(opposite) Nesting ducks near Moel y Don.

(above) Llanddwyn Island.
(opposite) Stepping stones at Afon Baint.

Hermon to Dwyran

Early morning sunshine and late afternoon gloom. From a bend in the road at Hermon, a small side road takes us to the shoreline. We are in awe of the wonderful houses along this stretch, envious of their view across the estuary. We even pass through the end of one of the gardens.

At Malltraeth and the marshes, crossing the Afon Cefni, we can easily see why the celebrated naturalist painter Charles Tunnicliffe chose to live here for over thirty years; the marshes and bay are teaming with birds.

Beyond is Newborough Forest, the largest public forest in Wales, it is noted for red squirrel conservation and we are hoping to spot one or two, but it isn't to be.

This is an extremely popular area with walkers. We abandon the path and head for the isolation of Penrhos beach – a vast expanse of golden sand. It's just ourselves, one man and a dog.

We check the tide tables and are able to walk directly across to Llanddwyn Island. This is such a special place. The church and well are dedicated to St Dwynwen, the Welsh patron saint of lovers. As the story goes, her father had marriage plans for Dwynwen which didn't coincide with her own. Dwynwen complained to God, and God turned Dwynwen's lover into a block of ice, but also gave Dwynwen three wishes. She wished to thaw the lover, for God to agree to meet the hopes and dreams of all true lovers, and that she be allowed to dedicate her life to God. In Wales, St Dwynwen's day is celebrated on January 25th, much in the same way as St Valentine is celebrated elsewhere on February fourteenth.

Onwards to Llanddwyn Beach, skirting the edge of the forest to get back on track. Frustrated, we allow ourselves a brief rant about signage, while knowing we were the ones to have strayed.

We do not access the main road at Pen Lon but detour to Llys Rhosyr. These historical ruins are linked to the medieval Princes of Wales. This is likely to have been one of the many courts, but the only one with visible remains. Llywelyn the Great (Llywelyn Fawr) certainly held court here

He ruled most of Wales for over forty years, and was of the eight hundred year long dynasty of the Kingdom of Gwynedd and House of Aberffraw.

We rejoin the path at Penlon, passing a pig farm, before turning right down a track leading to the giant stepping stones across the river Braint.

Two of the stones have moved and are now virtually triangular. At low tide, it is easier to take your shoes off and drop into the freezing cold water, rather than risk tumbling with camera and mobile phone into the river.

More muddy fields before reaching Dwyran, happy to get our boots off. The shock of the ice cold water of the river Braint had sorted out aching feet.

Egret on the river Braint.

St Cwyfan.

Rhosneigr and Hermon

Joined by our friend Louise, we start at the clock tower in Rhosneigr. According to Wikipedia it is the most expensive place to live on the island. A small bridge crosses the river, and the path heads diagonally through the dunes behind the Oystercatcher restaurant, beyond Traeth Llydan. Barclodiad y Gawres can be seen ahead on Mynydd Mawr. This is a prehistoric tomb, dated 2,500BC with carved stones. The tomb has been restored, but is locked as we pass. Guided tours can be arranged.

Rounding the bend, we come upon Porth Trecastell. The surfers are in the water, and the volunteer litter pickers are on the beach. Our friend Louise drops in for a chat.

At this stage, we are aware of the irritating whine of car engines as they race around the Anglesey circuit. It disturbs the tranquility of the day. Each to one's own in pursuit of enjoyment, but we prefer the tranquil!

At Porth Cwyfan we stop for lunch at another special place, looking out on St Cwyfan's Church in the Sea, a medieval church dating from the twelfth century, dedicated to the Irish St Kevin. It is probably the most photographed church on Anglesey, and it is not hard to see why as it is perched on the tiny Cribinau island encircled by a sea wall.

Oystercatcher.

The weather forecast has been for rain and we are gently steaming in our own personal sauna suits. I might shed a few more pounds. We feel a few drops of rain, but not even enough to dampen our sandwiches.

Moving on, we stop to watch the oystercatchers with their bright orange beaks, before following the river to Aberffraw, which had been the medieval capital of the Kingdom of Gwynedd, and the court of Llywelyn the Great. Edward I removed the stones from the court to build Beaumaris castle, then built the village over any remaining trace.

The best view of the day is across the estuary to Aberffraw beach, with the Llŷn coastline a deep blue in the background.

We cross over the old bridge, and to make up time, we take the high tide route to Hermon. By now we were thinking of the journey home.

As we drive across from the Isle of Anglesey onto the mainland the heavens open, and a rainbow smiles down, while it rains for the four hour drive to South Wales.

Anglesey sunset.

Rhosneiger to Rhoscolyn
Rhosneigr to Rhoscolyn with an unintentional side trip from Four Mile Bridge to Stanley Embankment.

The walk is clearly signposted from the centre of Rhosneigr and off the main road heading over a bridge at Afon Crigyll. It is a bright, sunny day. All is well with the world. We drop down to the beach at Traeth Cymyran. The path itself runs at a higher level, but the tide is out, and we opt for the sand

RAF Valley is based here, and you are left in no doubt by the numerous signs that you should keep moving and keep out.

Before turning off a sizeable track through a farmer's field, we stop to take in water and snacks. Louise is surprised by a pony sneaking up on her to steal her crisps. None of us hear that horse coming! We laugh, until we see the churned-up mud at the gate. Our boots are soon smelling of mulched manure.

Lucy turns to find another gateway!

We had already harmonized on an impromptu version of *What a Difference a Day Makes*, now Lucy and Louise have me in stitches, singing extracts from *The Sound of Music* with actions.

We follow the estuary up to Penrhyn-Hwlad, lying on the grass as we picnic, the sun on our faces. It is a nice feeling following such a long winter.

At Four Mile Bridge (so called, as it is four miles to Holyhead), we take the turning to the right off the bridge, as it was the only signpost direction and found ourselves unintentionally out on the Stanley Embankment.

Tiring, we walk across the Embankment to the car park and the convenient café at Penrhos Park.

We are debating whether we should give in for the day and try to get a taxi. The café owner overhears and says her husband will drop us off, wherever and whenever we are ready to go.

After a latté and a long break, we bundle into the pristine car in our muddy boots. On the drive we can easily see our mistake, and confusing our driver even further, we decide to resume our walk to Rhoscolyn from Four Mile Bridge.

He thinks it is madness to start again so late in the day and refuses payment for his efforts.

Once more on the path, we are startled by the sounds of a car horn. Our friend has returned to check we have the right directions and a map. I think he feels a sense of responsibility, particularly as we had dithered so much about our destination.

The kindness of strangers never ceases to amaze me.

The rest of the walk to Rhoscolyn is uneventful, and we return by car to our starting point at Rhosneigr for fish and chips at sunset.

Time to enjoy lunch with the pony.

Colourful Kayaks.

South Stack to Rhoscolyn

South Stack lighthouse stood out in the mist. We park at the RSPB site and head down to Elin's Tower, a folly built in 1868. Louise investigates the clifftop and is surprised by a birdwatcher who has already identified fifteen different species that morning.

I detour to the Ty Mawr Iron Age hut circles. Evidence suggests that these were lived in as far back as 500AD. The wonderfully named Abraham's Bosom Bay comes next. We spot some colourful kayaks out to sea, and meet up with them again at Porth Dafarch, a very pleasant sandy cove with benches and toilets. A great place to have a picnic.

The weather turns increasingly grey as we cross the busy beach at Trearddur Bay and head up towards the rocky shore. It becomes wet underfoot and bleak, but we have to stop to take in the natural white and black arches of Bwa Gwyn and Bwa Du.

Stopping to chat to a young climber, who is buddied up with a friend dangling down the cliff side in a very precarious fashion, we quickly traverse the moorland to Rhoscolyn. It is so misty we can barely see a trace of the offshore islands.

We ponder at the site of St Gwenfaen's Well. The waters are meant to cure mental problems. It is a mystery how many places become associated with legends and healing. Where did it all start?

Some legends along the coast are based on historic facts, some on superstition, some told by travelling bards, some by pilgrims. Wherever we

Trearddur Bay.

walk we value the legacy of these storytellers adding depth and colour to the geography of the landscape.

We become quite excited seeing a cromlech in the field by the car park, only to find out it was yet another folly!

On previous evenings we have failed miserably to get into two recommended restaurants. The Sospan and Butchers, a Michelin restaurant in Menai Bridge was full for the next six months. The Marram Grass near Newborough was also bursting at the seams. Tonight we happily settle for a drink at the White Eagle Inn, Rhoscolyn, said to be a favourite of Prince William during his time on Anglesey. Followed by dinner at the Shanty Café in Trearddur Bay. A satisfactory end to a grey day.

St Cybi's Church.

Penrhos and South Stack

Penrhos is a pleasant starting point to any walk. We look out for red squirrels at the feeding boxes in the park, then cut through the pet cemetery – nothing to do with Stephen King's creation, but a place of rest for beloved family pets. The walk is easy going at this stage, passing the ruins of a naval battery dating from the Napoleonic wars, along the shoreline, until we turn towards the urban sprawl of Holyhead.

We stop and watch a training rescue exercise out to sea. We look up at the Skinners Monument (an obelisk on the hilltop), but are not tempted to climb up for a closer look. We have a long day ahead!

The path signs through Holyhead are a bit scarce. We take out the guidebook, which points us in the direction of the station, across the Millennium Bridge (or the Celtic Gateway Bridge) towards the town centre and St Cybi's church.

Holyhead in Welsh is *Caer Gybi*. The fortress walls surrounding the church date from Roman times, and the original church was built in 520 AD. The social history recorded on the gravestones show numerous young deaths. I am sobered by the tragedy some families seem to have suffered. Was it cholera, Spanish Flu or disaster at sea? The local historian is busy with an American tourist and we didn't have time to wait.

Along the shoreline we stop to chat to a knowledgeable chap on his bike. He tells us of the terrible damage done by Storm Emma in March 2018. Indeed, we could still see some traces of boats in the harbour as we walk

South Stack.

onwards passing the Soldiers Point House. Reaching the foreshore, where the damaged boats had been brought ashore, we can see for ourselves the millions of pounds worth of damage that has taken place.

The path tends to get a bit tricky as we head uphill, towards the quarry face. Top marks though to Anglesey Coast Path for the work done on the path surface and the coded numbers on benches, etc. In the event of an emergency, these are clear location markers. From here we scramble up the path towards the North Stack fog warning stations. Great views back towards the Holyhead breakwater, reputedly the largest in the UK, stretching out like a giant serpent into the sea.

A choice of rocky paths presents themselves. We don't go up to the summit of Holy Mountain, but there is the feel of a pilgrimage route to this section – a timeless quality. As we walk over hard rock we find it is interlaced with tumbling heather. It cannot have changed much through the centuries.

The final stretch is a very pleasant walk, made perfect by the spring sunshine, zig zagging our way towards the South Stack Lighthouse, iconic and familiar from several tourist publications and images. This is followed by a further stroll to the RSPB car park.

Bridge over river Alaw.

Penrhos and Church Bay

I t may be worth stating that the Isle of Anglesey Coast Path (2006) has been around longer than the Wales Coast Path (2012). There seems to be constant improvements, so we abandon the guidebooks and download the information from the www.anglesey.gov.uk website, which seems to be regularly updated. The angles of the Anglesey signage sometimes seem to be strange, but we put that down to our interpretation.

We are back in the car park in Penrhos Coastal Park. We wanted to pop into the Toll House Café to tell the owners that we had survived the walk to Rhoscolyn. The owner had helped us out with a lift during a previous walk. He must have been quite concerned to see these vague, confused women heading out into the gloom.

It is a bit like *Groundhog Day* as we cross the Stanley Embankment. Designed by Thomas Telford to improve links between Dublin, Holyhead and London, it links the Isle of Anglesey with Holy Island. The two islands are separated by the narrow Cymyran channel. Holy Island is so-called due to the number of standing stones and burial chambers. It is accessed by our twice travelled Stanley Embankment, named after the Stanley family, who were local benefactors.

I mention to Lucy that Dawn French was born on the island in Holyhead, while her dad was in the services. This gets us talking about who we would like to play us, should we have a movie made of our lives. We eventually settle on Joanna Lumley and Jennifer Saunders.

We turn down the path by a garage to find the seaweed-covered Gorad Beach while the tide is out. We then turn inland towards the Afon Alaw estuary. There is a fancy new bridge crossing the river before you reach Llanfachraeth. The weather turns nasty here, with squally showers, obliterating any views across to Holyhead, but it clears by the time we reach Traeth y Gribin.

At Penrhyn Bay the path goes through the caravan park, but it is possible to walk across the beach. There is a shop and café on the site though. It seems a good idea to top up with refreshments, as there will be little opportunity further up the coast.

Another sandy bay at Porth Tywyn Mawr, and apart from some muddy fields the path continues smoothly to join a road, then off the road again towards Trwyn Gwter-fudr (Dirty gutter nose), Cable bay and then Porth Swtan (Whiting Port) more commonly called Church Bay, with its café and Lobster Pot restaurant.

An old boat on the shore.

Porth Swtan.

Church Bay and Cemaes

Early morning, we meet with our good friends Esther and Judith and explore the grounds of the Swtan Heritage Museum, a restored seventeenth century Welsh cottage, which unfortunately doesn't open until the second bank holiday in May, so we don't linger.

We set off at a brisk pace gradually going uphill towards Porth y Bribys. We stop to consider our next steps as there are fences and signs intermingled, plus lots of cows in the field. We eventually make our way past the cows, down an incline to the little island Ynys y Fydlyn, with a freshwater lake beyond.

We stop for a breather before scrambling up the cliff face and some rocky terrain which levels off as we approach the abandoned copper works and the two navigational points known as the White Ladies.

Out to sea the Skerries Lighthouse dominates the horizon, a reminder of the treacherous seas around Anglesey, and the numerous shipwrecks and lives lost. A sobering thought.

Even more sobering is the sight of Wylfa Nuclear Power Station. The juxtaposition against the rural scenes of sheep grazing and farmers tilling the fields is altogether a bizarre sight.

We sidetrack from here to visit the little church in the field beyond and make our way across the Mynachdy estate, dropping slightly to Hen Borth then rounding Trwyn Cemlyn, followed by a hard slog across the shingle on Cemlyn Bay. We stop to talk to some wardens from the reserve. They are

Cemaes.

watching out for incoming birds, mainly terns. Rather them than us, as there is a fresh, cool breeze blowing.

At the Felinheli Cafnan corn mill, we take a break. It is situated in a little dip, out of the wind. We wash our boots in the clear water. They certainly have collected some mud during the walk.

Back on track we are soon trying to negotiate our way around Wylfa. There is a sign discarded in the bushes leading to the forest, but that path is overgrown. We walk around Wylfa following the roadway keeping a wary eye open for any signs. It feels strange, soulless and not the most endearing part of the walk. We eventually climb over a gateway to get out of the area.

We quickly make our way towards Cemaes Head, stopping for a bar meal at the Stag pub, some visitors have been in the bar all day. We don't linger. Four tired ladies make their way to the car passing Harry Furlong Buoy, which now stands to one side on the Main Street to the harbour, rather than warning ships against the danger of the rocks at Trwyn Cemlyn.

The sun shines on the pretty little harbour of Cemaes.

Cemaes and Amlwch Port

This turns out to be one of my favourite walks. In addition to the natural beauty, there is a wealth of easy-to-access heritage sites. We set off across the harbour stopping to take in the Tide and Time St Patrick's Bell, before heading for the headland.

Reaching Porth Padrig beach, the rock formation Y Ladi Wen/The White Lady stands out against the backdrop of the golden cliffs. No wonder Anglesey is a joy for geologist field trips and hardly surprising that the island is part of the European Geoparks Network and the Global Geoparks Network.

We walk across the beach and scramble up the other side. Our next stop is the enchanting Llanbadrig Church. Named after St Patrick, who is said to have been shipwrecked on the island.

There has been a church on the site since 440AD. This simple church is a tranquil stop off point.

Climbing over the stile in the churchyard, we make out the hazy outline of the Isle of Man. From here, the walk gets more strenuous, with steep steps to Porth Llanlleiana. The clay works here were built over a nunnery; porcelain was created here until it closed in the 1920s.

We choose to stick to the more strenuous route rather than divert to an easier stretch, and continue to Hell's Mouth – Porth Cynfor, another steep descent and ascent!

Moving swiftly on, we are fascinated by the completeness of the Borth Wen brickworks, from the ruined winding gear on the hill to the chimneys and kilns. It also features a natural arch that looks like an elephant's trunk.

From here there is a nice, easy section to Bull's Bay, the rocks here are over six hundred million years old, which is how old we are beginning to feel. We watch a group of rowers in the bay, before pushing on to Amlwch, and are happy to see the bromide extraction plant come into view. It is the end to our brilliant day's walking.

St Patrick's Bell sign.

Rough hewn steps well-trodden over time.

Dulas to Amlwch Port

The air is still damp after the night's rain. A gloomy start to the day but we have various options on the walk should the heavens open. We are staying at a small cottage on the outskirts of the Amlwch Port, conveniently placed for the planned walks.

The dank atmosphere is enhanced by the hull of a rotting wrecked boat at the estuary of Afon Goch, (Red River) – it wasn't a day to linger as we carried briskly onwards. I totally dislike the damp.

Leaving the estuary, we work out the way around the large, private estate. A reminder of how complex the task of creating the Anglesey Coast Path would have been, ensuring that the wishes of landowners were considered as well as forging a memorable coastal walk. Not easy.

A flurry of pheasants adorn not only the fields, but also some had ventured into the graveyard at Gwenllwyfo church, no doubt enjoying the peace and quiet.

The weather brightens as we enter the fields with the spring lambs looking at us with curiosity.

Out to sea there are two rocky crags. Ynys y Carcharorion (the island of prisoners) where it is said that prisoners were tied up until the tides took them. The other, with a small tower, where apparently the lady of the manor used to make sure that supplies were left on this island just in case shipwrecked sailors were washed up on its shore. Evidence of purgatory and philanthropy in one viewpoint.

Towards Trwyn Elian Lighthouse, the heathland is bright yellow with gorse. It has a sense of the remote. Like Beaumaris Castle, this lighthouse is also squat against the landscape. It was built by the Liverpool Dock company in the eighteenth century to help their ships navigate these waters safely.

A short road walk towards Porth Elian, before traversing along the clifftops eventually dropping down to the holy well at Ffynnon Elian. It is said that the sixth century saint Elian was thirsty and prayed for water, and lo and behold the water flowed.

We move inland towards a sad looking house; we are approaching Amlwch Port, where copper was transported from the nearby copper mines of Parys mountain.

We head to our little cottage for a late lunch, and we plan the next stage of our Anglesey walk.

Ffynnon Elian holy well.

Coxswain Richard 'Dic' Evans at Moelfre.

Travelling between Llanddona and Dulas

As we drive down to Llanddona beach from the village we hold our breath. The road is winding, narrow and steep. It is early morning and promises to be a glorious day.

The tide is out. Esther has driven across from North Wales to join us on our penultimate walk. We set off along the beach, before heading back to the signposted path over the marshes. This is a glorious curve of coast to Red Wharf Bay and most of it follows the shoreline. We go over the little bridge, before rounding the curve and stopping off for coffee at The Ship Inn, already terribly busy despite the early hour.

Esther is a font of local knowledge and tells us that the concept for the original Land Rover off-road vehicle for farmers was created here. The iconic British brand was the brainchild of Maurice Wilks, a chief engineer at Rover, who had a farm on Anglesey and is said to have outlined his plans on this very beach.

For some reason, whenever I pronounced Red Wharf Bay it came out as Red Dwarf Bay and so it shall be forever more. Passing by the car park, we continued to the end of the road, where the signpost takes us up the hill through a caravan park. Towards the end of the site, we fork off to the right of the main road. We miss a low level sign and find ourselves in a new luxury chalet development called the View, which we don't have time to enjoy. We realise our mistake and retrace our steps downhill.

For the first time in months, we feel hot under the noon day sun – just saying, not complaining. We reach the wooded path with glimpses of clear blue sea; a large limestone quarry face towers above us on the left of the path. We step onto the road at Benllech and stop for our picnic lunch on the benches facing the beach. Families are out enjoying the Early May Bank Holiday sun.

Following a diversion, we end up in a caravan park. There has been a significant cliff fall. The three of us aimlessly try to find a way out and onwards. We are helped on our way by a kind chap popping out of his caravan and, encouraged by the 'Missus', he walks with us until we are back on track. The signs are discreet to say the least.

This is followed by a very relaxing walk onwards through Traeth Bychan and Penrhyn Point, with crystal clear blue water on our right.

Moelfre is our next stop; tea and cake at Ann's Pantry beckon. A group of ladies are enjoying a long lunch. As they open their fourth bottle of Prosecco we drool with envy!

We walk across the front, up to the wool shop that Esther used to visit, while holidaying with her aunt as a child. Happy memories. Passing below the commemorative statue to coxswain, Richard 'Dic' Evans awarded the RNLI gold medal, having served on one hundred and seventy-nine launches and saved two hundred and eighty lives.

After the lifeboat station we cover some ground across the clifftops, stopping to take in the Royal Charter Memorial just above the path. This clipper was on the last leg of its journey from Melbourne to Liverpool in October 1859 when it went aground. In a hurricane force twelve storm, four hundred and sixty lives were lost, along with the cargo. There was a great deal of gold on board, and the largest gold nugget found on Anglesey was discovered as late as 2012.

An easy walk to yet another sandy beach at Traeth Lligwy. A couple walk past; the lady is wearing white, fluffy mules in total contrast with our muddy booted selves. The car park is packed with camper vans, through the sandy dunes we go towards Traeth yr Ora. You can go down to the beach, but our path turns inland.

We then follow the path inland for quite a long stretch, before eventually reaching a small pond. Continuing to the right of the pond we make our way wearily to the Pilot Boat Inn on the A5025 in Dulas.

Through the mist we completed the eight hundred and seventy mile walk on Llanddona Beach.

Beaumaris to Llanddona

Here we are at last; the final day's walking on the Wales Coast Path. We are up early only to be greeted by a dense sea fog. By the time we position our cars and set off along the promenade in Beaumaris, there is enough visibility to walk, but not enough to see the glorious views across the bay.

Beaumaris Castle is a vague, ghostly outline in the distance. From the promenade we enter a kissing gate, which leads us up through a grassy field. We stop to talk to a chap who is hoping for the fog to lift. We tell him that by the end of the day we will have walked the eight hundred and seventy miles of the Wales Coast Path. He is full of admiration and wants to know what charity we are supporting so he could donate. Several people had offered to donate to a charity of our choice en route, but we hadn't really considered the option.

Once off the grassy path, we follow the road clearly signposted onto a concrete wall, then a shingle beach. We try to find some sandy bits as the shingle is hard work. Should anybody be looking out from the houses, we are probably a sorry sight as we scrunch our way along delicately in the mist.

Along the cliff face, caves appear to have been dug out, while one boulder looks like an ugly giant's face, alongside an isolated rock formation.

Before we are forced off the beach by a river running through, we stop to take in the big reveal. The mist has lifted a little and we get a brief view of Snowdonia in the distance. Tantalising!

We head inland following the signs to steps, another shingle beach and yet another long stretch by road to the eleventh century Penmon Priory. In his time Llywelyn Fawr supported the church, but it had much faded by the sixteenth century when Henry VIII, and his Dissolution of the Monasteries Act, finished it off. The two tenth century crosses from the monastery are still in the church. A healing well, Priory House and a distinctive dovecote, which dates from the Elizabethan era, completes the historic site. A film featuring Angelina Jolie and Vanessa Redgrave called *The Fever* was made here in 2003.

There is a quirky Toll Gate up to Trwyn Du and the Penmon Lighthouse, charging motorists and overnight campers. Still draped in mist, we can see across to Puffin island, home to thousands of puffins and guillemots. On a good day you can see Llandudno and the Isle of Man.

The camper vans parked here for the night are getting ready to set off for the day, while we make our way to the whitewashed café for a cuppa.

The Wales Coast Path turns left, just before the car park and is clearly signposted, until you reach a long whitish wall, and we are signposted downhill...

From here we lose track of directions, and just follow the route around and between white-washed houses, over narrow roads and wooded track to Glan-yr-Afon.

We are reminiscing about our walk so much we miss a sign. While the guidebooks talk about Llanfihangel Chapel we find ourselves at Llanfihangel School, but we soon spot the working farm, which is mentioned in the guidebook.

Blimey, I must be tired. I leave my camera on the wall while checking the onward journey. Once I spot this, I race back to collect it; the camera has been like an extra limb throughout this adventure.

Some great work has taken place here to amend the route, but our guidebook doesn't follow the new layout. There is a steep descent down some steps. We hope this would end the eight hundred and seventy mile walk.

I spot a local fisherman on the beach. He is happy to take our photo. Lucy isn't too keen (by this stage her feet are blistered and we are both dog-tired).

Looking back, we are glad we had that one picture to commemorate walking the whole length of the Wales Coast Path in our very slow, haphazard, pleasurable way.

We have met some wonderful walkers with a passion for the outdoors, and the kindest of locals who have helped us on our way.

We savour a moment of euphoria, before we jump in the car to take on that testing road up to Llanddona village. In Beaumaris, where the mist still hangs around the harbour, I allow myself a few tears of joy, before jumping into my car and beginning the four hour drive home, musing about our hundred days, not of solitude, but of slow walking on the Wales Coast Path.

REFLECTION – *MYFYRDOD*

Here we are at the end of our eight hundred and seventy mile journey on foot. Little do we realise that in a short time our freedom will be curtailed by a global pandemic. Our strolls today are round trips starting and finishing at home. The golden age – when we made it up as we went along, striding out at dawn for remote spots on the Wales Coast Path, visiting local attractions and restaurants along the way – is, for now, a thing of the past, or at least it will not happen without some serious additional planning.

My friends and family have told me numerous times that Lucy and I have a story to tell, and without a doubt the hero of the story is the Wales Coast Path.

The decision to walk the eight hundred and seventy miles did not come easy. Numerous excuses came to mind. It would take time; it would take planning. I was not fit. I was of an age where most people would designate me to the sofa, with a cup of tea/glass of wine, soap operas and slippers. I also knew that once Lucy got the bit between her teeth, she would be tenacious about completing our journey, and I wouldn't want to let her down. While I, on the other hand, had a low boredom threshold and how would the Wales Coast Path sustain my interest for one hundred days? Did I have the staying power?

Once started, I became obsessed with the Wales Coast Path – this gorgeous girdle, laced in the legends and history that surround Wales. I couldn't wait to get out there for the next session. I carried my camera and, at night, completed my journal. It became a way of life.

Two mile strolls became five mile hikes, daily walks led to overnight stays, slowly but surely, we built our stamina to fifteen miles and inched our way around our marvellous coast. I occasionally fibbed about the distances we were walking in a day. Lucy was well able to walk long distances, but hated the thought of stretches over ten miles. Lucy knew I fibbed because I couldn't meet her eye, but sometimes a slight evasion got results.

On any walk it takes time to get into the rhythm, or to the head space where your day-to-day problems are left behind. There comes a stage where you just soak up the scenery, and not really being aware of the distance travelled, or how far we have left to go. Walking the Wales Coast Path is a masterclass in mindfulness. Some days we talked furiously and on others it would be complete silence, but on every walking day, for at least some part of that day, the Path world took over sharing its wonder, cleansing and healing the mind. These are the times that I can powerfully recall and use to counteract the many frustrations that we face today.

If I were to give advice to novice walkers. It would be:

Find a compatible walking companion. Lucy and I had known each other a long time. We can chat for Wales, on mostly any subject, but back off quickly when recognising the other's need for silence. She would ignore me when I got frustrated at missing a sign or having to backtrack. I would, in turn, become very hearty when we were both visibly tiring. 'Almost there' and 'Not far to go now'. I also knew if Lucy's shoulders drooped, and she started walking at a fast pace, she wanted the walk to come to an end, and it was best to stay quiet.

Both Lucy and I are slow walkers. We don't rush or race to the end destination. That doesn't mean to say we didn't have long days, but early starts or late finishes compensated for our preferred pace and intense appreciation of the coast.

Agree your roles: I would plan the walking sections, where we would meet, where we would leave our cars for the day, local transport if any available. The length of the walk depending on terrain, the weather forecast, etc. Lucy would sort out the accommodation, where we would dine out, and any local event that would coincide with our walk. We would talk through any complications prior to booking or setting off. We had a wish list for our accommodation requirements which included, off road parking, Wi-Fi, a bath and a shower. The location needed to be where it would make most logical sense for the walking sections, also where we could easily access a restaurant or any other local experience and social interaction at the end of the day.

Add friends to the mix: Get them to join you for the walks. When spirits are flagging, they bring energy and boost your morale.

Sort out your wardrobe: It took us a while to get the right walking gear. Boots and wet weather gear were the biggest consideration. We layered up so that we could easily strip if we were getting too hot. I walked in wellingtons, boots and walking shoes, but never walking sandals, and spare socks were a must.

Be aware: since we have walked the Wales Coast Path there has been erosion, new layouts, and the Green Bridge of Wales has had big rocks drop into the sea. The path is a fantastic asset for Wales, but the environment is evolving and erosion is clear along the path.

Carry provisions: Make sure you have ample water and food for the walk, particularly in more isolated spots. If near a village shop locally, stop for a snack in a café or bar and enjoy talking to the locals.

Sing your heart out: In forests it could be *Take Me Back to the Black Hills*. On the coast it could be *We are Sailing, Yellow Submarine* or extracts from *The Sound of Music* coupled with some Welsh Rugby Songs, *Ar Lan Y Mor* or hymns.

Enjoy the history as well as the landscape: Each section has a different story to tell, this kept me engrossed as much as the scenery.

Wine and Dine locally: However tired, go out and enjoy what is available. It is what slow walking is about, the locals will love to know more about you, and they will enjoy sharing local knowledge, and a bit of gossip, now and then.

Budgeting: The question we have both been asked since we completed our walk is how much did you spend? We didn't keep track. We had a joint kitty purse and when it was empty we topped it up. Lucy was far more entrepreneurial. While we were on our short breaks, she would rent her place out on AirBNB thus offsetting any costs for accommodation. We shopped in little local grocery stores and dined out where we could or catered for ourselves as most of the time we opted for self-catering accommodation.

When I was growing up my father would say, 'You can be anything you want to be. You can do whatever you want to do. Only you can make it happen.'

My father was right. I slow walked the Wales Coast Path, and we found a way to make it happen from baby steps, local walks of two or three miles, to giant strides of fifteen to twenty miles. I wouldn't have believed it possible, and I certainly wouldn't have persevered without my pal, Lucy, with her indefatigable spirit and humour egging me on to the finishing stretch.

For me, Lucy, the co-walker it has been quite an experience. The walk did become an obsession and the trick for me was not to over think things because therein lies thousands of reasons and excuses not to carry on.

A friend joined us on one of the walks and asked how we worked out where to start every day. I looked at her with astonishment and said, 'Well, from where we ended the day before of course.'

I would return home and tell my mother, sister and friends that I had the edge on a mountain goat and my new name was Forrest Gump. They had many a laugh at my expense.

It was fantastic to have such a focus, such freedom to travel and tour, such good health and company. It is at such times that life and thinking move forward.

We had moments of glory…

We are in the Hall of Fame on the Wales Coast Path website. We were made nature ambassadors for the National Trust and now hopefully have captured the sense of adventure in a book.

And there will always be memories of a landscape, a clear sky and mind.

I searched high and low for a painting that would capture the glory and sometimes the pain of the walk, and eventually hit upon Carys Bryn and the picture below which she named for me *poen plesurus* – a painful pleasure.

I also had to own the gaps in my own knowledge about Welsh history and culture. Since the walk I have enjoyed learning to speak Welsh with confidence and have become a professional Welsh tourist guide.

All roads lead somewhere.

Mae'r holl ffyrdd yn arwain rhywle.

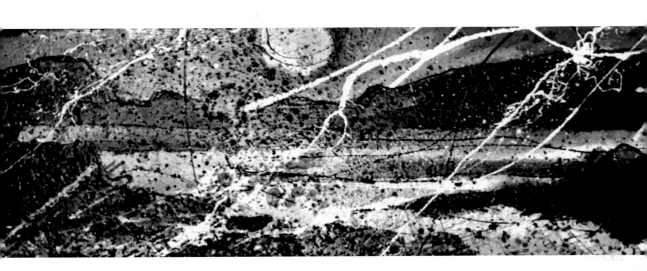

ACKNOWLEDGEMENTS – CYDNABYDDIAETH

We are grateful to all the agencies and individuals who were responsible for the concept, delivery and ongoing maintenance of the Wales Coast Path. A huge thank you to the guidebooks, websites, applications, blogs, interpretation panels, and the friends and family for helping us reach our goal. Without their expertise and support we would not have completed our slow walk along the Wales Coast Path.

These are the reference materials we returned to again and again for information for and on our journey. To access a wide range of useful information on the Wales Coast Path please refer to: *www.walescoastpath.gov.uk* and download the app. The interactive maps are particularly useful in preplanning.

Walking the Wales Coast Path – Paddy Dillon published by Cicerone.

The Wales Coast Path – A Practical Guide for Walkers – Christopher Goddard & Katharine Evans published by St David's Press.

Wales: A Physical, Historical and Regional Geography by E G Bowen published in 1957 by Methuen.

Blue Guide Wales
Lonely Planet Wales.

www.cadw.gov.wales
www.nationaltrust.org.uk
For the blogging walkers that had gone before and their invaluable insights, but mainly to Charleshawes.veddw.com
For sheer guts and inspiration: *onewomanwalkingwales.com*

This picture by North Wales artist Carys Bryn visually represents the emotion and the challenge of the Wales Coast Path. *Poen Pleserus* – pleasurable pain is an apt title.

We discovered much about Wales, the coast, its history and its people. As novice walkers we set about identifying start and finishing points compatible with our physical fitness, learning to adapt as we became more proficient.

We hope you enjoyed the journey.